DAMARIS PARKER-RHODES

# The Way Out is the Way In

'Remember that you are at an exceptional hour in a unique epoch, that you have this great happiness, this invaluable privilege, of being present at the birth of a new world'
—*The Mother (Sri Aurobindo Ashram)*

QUAKER HOME SERVICE
LONDON

First published May 1985
by Quaker Home Service
Friends House, Euston Road, London NW1 2BJ

© Damaris Parker-Rhodes, 1985
ISBN 0 85245 187 3

Cover design by John Blamires

Printed in Great Britain in Linotype Times 10/12
by Headley Brothers Ltd., Invicta Press,
Ashford, Kent and London

# Contents

# Acknowledgements

I wish to thank Dorothy Emmet, Jim Garrison and Frederick Parker-Rhodes for going through this book at various stages, and making valuable suggestions. I am also indebted to Eric Hutchison in a very special way, and above all to David Blamires who at a really busy time took on the job of cleaning up the whole manuscript. I want also to thank my University of the Third Age group and my Wednesday Women's group for making suggestions and above all for listening.

DAMARIS PARKER-RHODES

# PREFACE

Damaris Parker-Rhodes is well-known among Quakers in Britain; there can be few areas of the country where she has not spoken to groups of Friends or to public meetings on various aspects of spiritual experience and social concern. She has brought, and still brings, inspiration and encouragement to many through the intense honesty and emotional vigour with which she has shared her religious struggles and insights. In 1977 she was invited to encapsulate the stages of her spiritual journey in the Swarthmore Lecture, an occasion in the Quaker year when a leading Friend has the opportunity to expound his or her view of some of the fundamentals of Quakerism before a large public audience. This was published as *Truth: a Path and not a Possession*[1] and became one of the best-sellers among Quaker publications; it is now out of print. The present volume, *The Way Out is the Way In*, fills the gap in providing a much fuller and more strongly personal account of Damaris's spiritual quest.

Spiritual autobiography is a rare phenomenon in our times. In order to be of real value, it must go deep and not avoid pain, suffering and death. In the honest grappling with certainties and uncertainties we can recognize the truth of the psalmist's words:

> Deep calleth unto deep at the noise of thy waterspouts: all thy waves and thy billows are gone over me.
> Yet the Lord will command his lovingkindness in the daytime, and in the night his song shall be with me, and my prayer unto the God of my life.

Damaris's quest has led her in directions that some readers, both Quaker and otherwise, may think strange, but spiritual

1

power and truth flows strongly in channels that traditional Quakers and other Christians may find unfamiliar. However, the Quaker *Advices and Queries*,[2] guidelines revised in every generation, ask us: 'Are you loyal to the truth; and do you keep your mind open to new light, from whatever quarter it may arise?' Early Friends too were anxious not to restrict the activity of the spirit of Christ simply to those who knew his name, but had a more open, generous and loving view of the ways in which divinity reveals itself to humankind. Damaris's involvement with differing schools of meditation, prayer and spiritual practice, her sense of enrichment from both Quaker and Anglican worship, her encounters with deprived people and the drug-culture of the 1960s and 70s, her recognition of feminist thinking and exploration of the unity of body and spirit in health and growth—all these things can teach us more about the way the Holy Spirit is manifesting itself in the late twentieth century.

This book was written in the first place with Quakers in mind, but there must be many non-Quakers who will find stimulation and food for reflexion in its pages. For them a brief note on Quakerism may be in order.

The Religious Society of Friends (Quakers) grew up in the mid-seventeenth century as a reaction against the rigidities of both the Established Church and Puritanism. It has changed a great deal since the early days of Friends like George Fox and William Penn, but its form of worship today is still based on silent waiting upon God, out of which any worshipper may feel him- or herself called to speak words of personal experience, comfort, encouragement or thankfulness, perhaps to read from the Bible or to pray. The responsibility for worship lies on all present in the meeting, men, women and children alike, though people with known experience are appointed as elders and overseers for limited periods to exercise a special care respectively for the spiritual and pastoral welfare of those who form the meeting. All responsibilities in Quaker worship, service or business meetings may be undertaken by men and women alike.

The organizational structure of the Society provides for regular links of mutual responsibility between groups of Friends at local, regional and national levels. The national body of Quakers in Britain is known as London Yearly Meeting and meets once a year for conference and deliberation for a period of a few days; all members are entitled to attend. The ongoing work of the Yearly Meeting is discharged by a national representative council called, for historical reasons, the Meeting for Sufferings, and also by several committees appointed by it. The committees deal with such major concerns as peace, international service, social witness, education, the fostering of local meetings, publicity and the promotion of Quaker literature. Many other informal groups and committees exist to further more specialized interests. London Yearly Meeting is a very small religious body in relation to the total population of Great Britain; it numbers about 18,000 members, to which may be added about double that number of others who attend Quaker meetings more or less regularly.

Quakers are theologically liberal in outlook, undogmatic as regards matters of Christian belief and insistent on the primacy of personal experience. Among them are to be found individuals at many stages on the spiritual journey, some with a firm, simple Christian commitment akin to that of mainstream churches, while others have an openness of approach that may seem venturesome or foolhardy; all are held together by mutual tolerance and respect. Quakerism is, above all, a way of life rather than a system of beliefs, and in walking along that way our individual discoveries are augmented, modified, corrected and refined by those preceding and accompanying us.

For some people the way through life is relatively straightforward, but there are many for whom it is a labyrinth full of puzzles, dead ends and alternative routes with no guarantee of a successful outcome. For centuries men and women of all religions have sought to help others by writing down the twists and turns of their experience, the failings and barren times no less than the heights and the joy of divine love. Many Friends, especially in the seventeenth and eighteenth centuries, wrote journals and spiritual autobiographies which, despite social changes and altered philosophical and theological outlooks, may still inspire and illuminate us today. That practice is virtually dead now, but there is a continuing hunger for spiritual guidance, a desire to learn the raw truth about the religious quest. Damaris Parker-Rhodes's autobiography is not out to provide answers for everybody; it is the sharply focused account of one woman's life, not systematic, but keenly intuitive, daring to try things that most of us could hardly dare contemplate. It is an account of what the fourth section of the Quaker *Advices* counsels us to do in all simplicity and directness:

> Bring the whole of your daily life under the ordering of the spirit of Christ. Live adventurously. In every situation seek to be aware of the presence of God, praying that spiritual energies in yourself and in others may be released for the furtherance of God's kingdom.

DAVID BLAMIRES

# INTRODUCTION

It has taken me a long time to understand that a New Paradigm* is being born and that our culture-patterns, which have gradually been breaking up over my life-time, are now crystallizing into new ones. Time and again what I believed was my own revolutionary breakaway has turned out to be the same breakaway made by thousands of others. The spirit of the times seems to start work in certain of us from the moment we arrive on the scene; we are born with something new to say, and say it we must and will.

In this book, through the consideration of my own life-experience, I seek to understand how much of what has happened has been the planet striving to speak, using me as a point of awareness—as it were life living me rather than me living life. I am only too conscious that much has been wayward impulse, as though I have within me the kind of pressures that drives overpopulated lemmings to rush to the sea and drown themselves. At the same time I recognize impulses which derive from a higher consciousness than that of the thinking mind. This duality is true for society as a whole.

I feel more and more certain that the empowering of this new paradigm cannot come by active intellectual striving

---

* Thomas Kuhn used the term 'paradigm' in his book *The Structure of Scientific Revolution* (Chicago Univ. Press, 2nd edn, 1970) and it has been widely taken up. The word comes from *paradigma*, which is Greek for 'pattern'. It signifies a standard example against which theories are tested. When sufficient facts refuse to fit into this accepted framework, there comes upon society the need for what Kuhn called 'a paradigm shift'. At this point what has been blocking the waters of life cracks and renewal begins. Kuhn's primary consideration was of scientific theory, but very soon his idea permeated sociology, politics, health care, education and religion.

alone. The weight of all the contradictions which threaten to destroy life on earth is being accompanied by an outpouring of spiritual and mental power which makes wider and wider circles of enriched being possible to those who can channel them.

For instance, what was known as pertaining to saints long ago is now, over the past few years, being glimpsed by many more people, accompanied by charismatic healing, a seeing of the Inward Light and an increased sensing of the inward aspect hidden under the exterior of the material. Once it is understood that space and time, in which we normally function, are only an aspect of unlimited dimensions, then the way is open for the conscious channelling into the world of great reservoirs of peace and power. Meanwhile, there is only a narrow line between an awakening which causes us neurotically to dwell on the agonising facts of the world's danger and the quite different and positive path of quietly allowing a higher awareness to begin to permeate and remake our whole lifestyle. The point is to see ourselves as a part of planetary transformation.

Under the international and economic complexes which dominate, I have come to see more clearly that there is also a spider's web of human relationships which either supports or undermines all that happens. It is here that hope appears. As someone said to me recently: 'How on earth can you get these new ideas of peace and cooperation across to the people who matter?' The answer is that we are doing so far more than we yet realize. Our acts which often appear too insignificant to challenge the great machinations of history at this time are culminating in an enormous wave of inner being which is already drastically altering all the culture-patterns. The world itself is caught up in a crisis which will result either in its destruction or a break-through.

There is open revolt in many fields: this includes the demand for the end of the nuclear threat; the increased undermining of the remains of the reductionist scientific outlook; the rise of feminine anger and hope; the vision of a holistic approach to health and diet. Beyond all these aspects of new understanding is the realization that ecology must be planet-wide, because the world is an ecosystem. Alongside this are arising new conceptions of inner awareness, many of them bypassing the churches and rooted in psychology, physics and the application of science to psi-phenomena. East and West are meeting in exchange of techniques for the opening-up of the higher centres of consciousness. It is no longer unusual for a Christian to pursue an Eastern spiritual discipline or a humanist to practise Buddhist insight-meditation.

I have written this book in growing excitement, often lying awake at night pursuing fascinating conjectures and re-experiencing the past in the light of the new paradigm. This has felt like digging for treasure as I have begun to see new patterns emerging where before were only unrelated pieces. Certainly this has been no purely intellectual exercise, though I have been forced to allow the insights of our time, so far as I was able, to lead me forward. I have come to feel that my own life has been like a journey in mountain country, in and out of dark forests, along pleasant river valleys, often through deserts and occasionally up precipices with ropes and crampons—until momentarily I have reached a place where, the mists having cleared, I am able to glimpse the high tops and, looking back, see that all the time I have been travelling far more purposefully than I had realized—*because vast numbers of other people have been coming up the same way.*

This then is a salutation to fellow travellers, many of them way above me intellectually and spiritually, and a shout of celebration to those below, that the track actually leads somewhere and is clear for us to proceed.

DAMARIS PARKER-RHODES
Cambridge
October 1984

# CHAPTER 1

# LIFE IN TRANSFORMATION

**Transformation Crises**

I now see clearly that my basic life-pattern includes *transformation-crises*, which relate me to the transformation-crises in society and the world and are in fact an integral part of them.

Fortunately my roots run deep, both in the old Cornish family from which I sprang, in the (Anglican) Catholic Christian tradition, and in the Society of Friends, which I joined when I was just over thirty. This means that in the crazy swing of history on the move, I have always had the steadying influence of a secure background in feudalism, as well as membership of a well-based spiritual and social institution based on contemplation, fellowship and service. These have given me a dynamic point of integration for contraries which otherwise would have dragged me apart, so that while being carried along by circumstance, I have also become part of a transforming process.

I had an innate tendency to take traditional values seriously and in so doing have continually discovered myself challenging them. It was this that originally made it impossible for me to remain classbound, Conservative and Church of England. Being vigorous, I then went to the opposite extreme and for eight years belonged to the Communist Party. Leaving the Party and joining Quakers was for me finding the happy mean, and the Society provided a rock of security from which my spiritual and social investigativeness could set out on exploration. I consciously offered myself to life as a guinea-pig.

Since childhood I knew with certainty that there is *a within to every without*, though for a while I lost the connection by an over-emphasis on the intellectual when I was first married to my scientist husband and ardently embraced Marxism.

When I was eighteen I went to London for two years to take a secretarial training, followed by a job in an insurance firm. As a side-line I worked in the evenings with deprived children in a twilight area. My horror at the coldness and cruelty of London life and what I felt to be its denial of the brotherhood of man made me a socialist. In my Cornish village we were integrated with each other and our environment, and London brought alienation not only from the rhythm of the seasons and community living, but also from a part of my own nature. I see now that this experience was an echo of the growing plight of us all in the Western world, and increasingly over the planet too. If I suffered it more agonisingly than most, this was due to the fact that my home background provided so great a contrast.

Later I brought up a family, entered politics, was an active peace-worker, and helped to form the Cyrene organization that takes care of homeless people in Cambridge. For six years I was a County Councillor and held the position of first woman secretary to the Cambridge Council of Churches. It was against this background that my religious search through the years gradually opened into broader perspectives. I was fortunate to stumble across the writings of Berdyaev and Tillich (later so well summed up for me in John Robinson's writings) and further, by way of Eastern meditation and scriptures, the thought of C. G. Jung and Teilhard de Chardin.

As time has gone on I have come to view my Christianity as a spiritual/cultural development to be seen in the context of other faiths and world-wide. Theology I understand no longer as any absolute truth, but rather as the formulation of vitally poignant myth, ritual and poetry, by means of which we are enabled to relate to dimensions of being well beyond either reason or feeling.

In the sphere of faith I certainly see the process of the paradigm-shift at work. The 'big Daddy' God really is dead and has to rise again in fresh ways within the human psyche if we are to carry out our vocation of divinizing the earth. This is the task that reason by itself is unable to undertake. At the same time, the necessary mystical and poetic perception which makes it possible to experience what is beyond ordinary experience requires one to listen also to the mind. This paradox is part of the contraries by which we are forced to progress—often in agony of spirit.

Both my strength and also my limitation is that, having firm roots in the Catholic tradition which I found authenticated later in the silence of the Quaker meeting, when it comes to the crunch I cannot experience at depth *except* in and through its great archetypes. Thus in extremity its symbols prove to be my symbols and by them I am sustained.

When I am asked what I hold to be the most important facts that I know about life and its meaning, I tend to reply:

First, this is an *Incarnational World:* that is, it is in an evolutionary way becoming divinely aware of itself in and through humanity.

Second, our most dynamic archetype is *the Cross and Resurrection of Christ*, which pictures humanity becoming divine and the divine becoming human. This, a path of suffering and overcoming, implies an element in individual and social transformation which can be trusted to reveal precious potential.

My attraction to Quakers lay partly in the fact that they are naturally seekers. Over the years this communal delving has steadily provided me with support in daring to think and experience, both inwardly as well as politically and socially. A complementary contrast to this was my husband's and my membership of the Epiphany Philosophers, a group of scientists, philosophers, monastics and Quakers, who steadily over thirty years met four times a year in a windmill in Norfolk, to think out how science, philosophy and religion can fertilize each other towards a fundamental understanding of the world. In this very disciplined approach I trotted along behind trying to keep up, increasingly coming to realize that science and intuition need to be subject to one another. Again, Epiphany Philosopher thinking caused my husband, Frederick, perpetually to return from the University Library with the fruits of way-out research on the psychic, on dreams, hypnosis and charismatic healing, as well as his own special studies in modern physics and mathematics, to which he was contributing. At the same time we were meeting many healers, clairvoyants, psychics, as well as scientists who refused to separate their political and inner experience from their science.

It was natural therefore that the holistic approach in science should come our way also in its popular forms. Lyall Watson[3] opened up for me much that I had found too structured in other places, even if his rather uncritical use of sources might infuriate my husband. Seedcorn books for me were Fritjof Capra's *Tao of Physics* and his even better book, *The Turning Point*:[4] Marilyn Ferguson's compilation of New Age thinking, *The Aquarian Conspiracy*;[5] *Gaia, A New Look at Life on Earth*[6] by J. E. Lovelock, and *The Awakening Earth: Our Next Evolutionary Leap*[7] by Peter Russell. These coalesced my piecemeal approach into the realization that what I had been pursuing all my life in fact made a new pattern, which belonged to a fast inflowing tide of culture-transformation. I saw I was a drop in a great wave of being caused by the transformation required by the planet itself.

Alongside my membership of the Society of Friends I received precious teaching from many sources, including Transcendental Meditation, Theravada Buddhism and Sufism, until through meditation I began increasingly to experience that I was part of a world that was itself alive as part of *an Incredible Live Being*. This was a revelation, but also seemed to be something I had always known.

11

## Discovering Teilhard de Chardin

It is a well-known fact of experience that what one has come to understand is then fed back again as fact from the world. This then happened to me. From James Lovelock's book *Gaia, A New Look at Life on Earth*, I discovered that the planet behaves like a living system. The word *Gaia* comes from the Greek word for 'Earth Mother'. Lovelock's Gaia Hypothesis suggests that it *is* indeed a living system which is being 'manipulated on a day-to-day basis by the many living processes on Earth. The entire range of living matter on earth, from viruses to whales, from algae to oaks, plus the air, the oceans and the land-surfaces all appear to be part of a giant system able to control the temperature and the composition of the air, sea and soil, so as to maintain the optimum conditions for the survival of life on the planet'.[8]

Mother Nature has solved extraordinary problems on behalf of life many times. It appears that each catastrophe has acted as a pressure for the production of higher forms of life. Crisis is the seedbed for evolutionary leap. Now for the first time such crisis has to be made conscious: our man-made crisis requires a man-made solution.

All this material fitted in well with the mixture of science and mysticism I had discovered a little earlier in the writings of Teilhard de Chardin. Certainly man is *a Threshold* rather than *a Ceiling*. In the present crisis, either life on earth will fail or it will succeed, but in any case all is not lost. Ours is a tiny planet of a small star in a minor galaxy: Life certainly has other eggs in her basket. All the same, our development appears to be rare, beautiful and precious, and we are certainly the spearhead of evolution, which is now in the process of emergence in an extraordinary direction. By meditation and the reception, in an aware way, of spiritual energy an increasing number of people are directly experiencing a Newness—the Christ (or Atman) within.

12

At the beginning of the century Teilhard was, among others, realizing that the theory of evolution affected every sphere of thought and faith. Life is a process of becoming, and if we are not to be overtaken by it, we have to realize the importance both of the kind of research and the kind of mysticism that can increase awareness.

As Teilhard wrote, with the coming of humanity there emerged out of the Biosphere what he called *the Noosphere* —a conscious layer that can become aware of its unconscious background. And so a reflexive world, a world that can reflect itself, is born.

Evolution now progresses by means of communication, libraries, cybernetics, television and radio. As life had appeared at one critical point in evolution, so now this Noosphere appears at another critical point. Explosion of the phyla of the species had scattered life far and wide across the planet in an amazing interconnected network, and now the direction of evolution changes from *divergent to convergent.* Everything is being brought together, and *explosion* is becoming *implosion.*

Teilhard, in his book *The Future of Man,*[9] outlines three headings for examination of what is happening to us. The first is *Social Integration*—the study of how we can bring about Planetary Man (this includes economics, international cooperation for peace-studies and inter-racial harmony). Second, *Technological Integration*, in which we discover how best to interact with our non-human environment. Thirdly, *Psychological Development,* in which our own consciousness is to be studied as being in the process of development into higher consciousness. In fact since Teilhard's time all these kinds of research have been in full swing, and when at last public opinion tops the wave of realization that we must live differently, much of the preparatory research will have already been done.

Teilhard noted that throughout evolution there seems to

13

have been a process that he called *Compression*, that is, through the saturation of one layer the next layer arose. Were we not now being compressed into some kind of unity by the approach of *a saturated Noosphere*? That is by over-population, world-destroying weapons, pollution and threats arising from modern technology. From the viewpoint of religious faith that means:

> By means of all created things, without exception, the divine assails us, penetrates us and moulds us. We imagined it as distant and inaccessible, whereas in fact we live steeped in the burning layers . . . and the within of man may be seen simply as one experience of the property matter possesses through space and time.[10]

For Teilhard Jesus on the Cross is Us on the Cross too, and faith has to include the fact that this is not a dying world, but one on the road to Resurrection. Faced with the greatest evolutionary jump since life began, we have to understand that this will take place via direct human awareness. The day of the local Christ is over and Teilhard's contribution to a universal faith is the vision of the Cosmic Christ and the Christification of the world. The life of Jesus of Nazareth illustrates, by symbol and everyday human reality, the immense labour of the ages, in which little by little spirit arises from and illuminates matter. Teilhard sees the cross of Christ as *the* central transformation-symbol, present in every aspect of life, and in the light of it our personal suffering can be seen as an expression of the painful birth of the future within us. Teilhard's final conclusion is that science must come to the Omega of realization of the unity of all life, while the Omega of faith points at the energizing with Christic love of the entire Cosmos.

This sweeping vision of the 1920s fits in closely with the *Gaia Hypothesis*. On the other hand, it is true that the present plight of our planet gives rise to the thought, echoed in both

14

James Lovelock's and Peter Russell's writings, that there is an analogy between modern civilization and cancer:

> Technical civilization really does look like a rampant malignant growth blindly devouring its own ancestral host in a selfish act of consumption.[11]

So we are faced with two possibilities in this crisis of awareness: either the cancer will spread to destroy life on earth, or a new understanding of man's living unity with the rest of nature will increasingly be linked with spiritual energies to bring about a rebirth.

The mystics of all ages and traditions declare that the divine is in fact already in some ways victorious—and that we can taste this through the practices of the inner life. In a strange way, Heaven is Now, and there is nowhere to go and no desert to cross. In the abyss (present in each person as well as in every culture) there dwells the Creative One, in whom we live and move and have our being. The disintegration we are forced to suffer has within it also the potential of a holy undoing by which we may be remade at depth.

It is against a background of belief that life is in movement towards such an evolutionary advance that in this book I centre my thoughts on what have been for me key-points in understanding in a very practical and active way.

## Encountering Quakerism

When at nursery school age our boys started to crack Thurber-type jokes, my husband and I were amazed at the arising of something so foreign. This developed as years went by into attitudes which led one son to work on cartoon film-making for Monty Python's Flying Circus and another to unite his scientific research with an intense passion for inner experiment.

I suppose I also surprised my parents when, as a young child growing up in an old Cornish family, I began to ask, noisily

15

and in public, questions about the truths of faith and social class. At around eight I broke the unspoken social laws by winking at a choir-boy in church—one of our farm tenants' sons (who later became a professor of mathematics in America)—asserting to myself that there was no doubt we could be friends. My father caught me in the act and on returning home gave me a severe dressing-down. The incident doubly impressed itself on my mind because it turned out not to be a matter of irreverence as my father implied, because my mother (going to the heart of the matter as women will) pointed out that the vicar's son was seated next to my winkee and perhaps it was at him I had winked!

The spirit of the times starts work in some of us despite an unwilling background and parentage. After an Anglican convent upbringing I plunged out, liked so many, into the Socialist dream of a fairer world. In fact, faced with the contradictions in capitalist society with which I came face to face in the poverty of East End pre-war London, I became for eight years a Communist. However, this turned out not to be the Stalinist variety. Eventually as the war ended I got myself embroiled in matters of authenticity and truth-speaking (as did also my husband over the Lysenko controversy) and we so antagonized our Party branch that we left.

The departure left me momentarily destitute of all the hard-won social and mental security I had acquired, and this came about in a double-sided way. Not only was I demanding absolutes of truth-seeking (not lies!), but I found in an odd way I had lost a quality of the livingness of life. This culminated finally one day when (having handed over our three young children to my husband immediately on his return from work) I walked out over the Long Ashton Downs behind Bristol where we lived and, facing the sunset, found tears pouring down my cheeks. For a moment I could not discover the reason, and then it came to me that I was miserable *because I had lost the secret behind sunsets*. As I pondered on

16

this, it led me to realize that I had also lost the hidden quality in human faces (perhaps the most mysterious thing in the world).

It took me a long time to fight my way through into the recovery of that secret being which I had taken for granted in childhood, and to find a language which could express it. I was shut off from religion by a newly acquired and not very stable scientific and Freudian outlook, got by living side by side with a scientist husband. This, however, while preventing me from trying to interpret what I was seeking in the Christian terms with which I had grown up, encouraged me to pursue inner truth pragmatically. William Blake's rhyme helped:

Reason says 'Miracle'; Newton says 'Doubt',
Aye, That's the way to make all Nature out.
'Doubt, Doubt and don't believe without experiment'.
That is the very thing that Jesus meant,
When he said 'Only Believe! Believe and try!'
Try, try and never mind the Reason.[12]

Finally I had an inner experience which disclosed to me once again the inner life hidden under the outer framework, and after a couple of years of serious search[13] I was led on to attend Quaker Meetings. Fortunately, after a few months my husband followed, guided as much by study of the Tao-te-Ching as by curiosity as to what satisfaction I was finding there. Here we found a worshipping group that met on the basis of silence, and it was exactly the matter-of-factness of this Quaker way which appealed to us. I might (and often did) experience a way-out mystical void and then someone would rise to their feet and start to talk about the need for peace-work; or I could be thinking about politics and a word would be said engulfing me in a silence in which anything appeared possible from the miraculous to the uttermost of disintegration. The inner and outer among Friends is not seen as separate, and that for me is crucial: inner and outer are bound into one.

Quakers specially seem to attract teachers, social workers, scientists and those who are more aware than most of the dangers and possibilities in the trends in society. This suited our need and we plunged in and came to find a lasting home in the Society of Friends.

Eventually, however, after ten or twelve years, while the activities side of Quakers gave me a niche in peace-work, I found in myself an increasing spiritual hunger, and this finally drove me beyond the frontiers of the Society, to find help in reaching a potential within that I knew to be there. Others in our ranks were doing the same, and wherever I went searching (Transcendental Meditation, Theravada and Tibetan Buddhism, T'ai Chi Ch'uan, Sufism), I also found a sprinkling of Friends! Now, as the years have gone by, whole groups of Friends start to find one another in fringe organizations like the Open Letter Movement, the Universalists, and even the long-established Seekers—where their 'dangerous thoughts' may be shared. However, the Quaker road from the first has been one of daring to understand that:

All Truth is a shadow except the last, except the utmost; yet every Truth is true in its kind. It is substance in its own place, though it be but a shadow in another place (for it is but a reflection from an intenser substance); and the shadow is a true shadow, as the substance is a true substance.[14]

There is nothing cast iron about such a view. It breeds tolerance, and because we have no ministers, creeds or set services, there is room for experimentation without the feeling of being a heretic. It is no accident then that Friends have a higher percentage of scientists in their number than other Christian groups.

## Peace, Social Action and Truth

Time and circumstance moved on. I was deeply impressed to watch what was happening to my children, and they frightened as well as delighted me. From peace-work (one went to prison from the same demonstration that I did) they proceeded to embrace the Beat Movement in a very conscious way, one seriously investigating the drug culture from inside (seriously, because he became a pharmacologist and did an M.Sc. on the effects of marijuana on the brain). They defied the sex mores we had tried to pass on to them and threw over any religious belief. In all this, however, there was an underlying quality of search, which was not simply chaotic.

Via the peace movement of the 60s (I was secretary for CND for East Anglia for a time and then had the paid secretary living in our house) I was in touch with numerous young people so that I knew quite well that our own family were part of a social movement. Under this shout of NO, the rising generation were proclaiming a hesitant and more positive answer. *It is this answer I believe which is now providing the beginnings of the New Paradigm.*

Marcuse's writing had, in an alarming way, challenged the liberal attitudes of people like us. By our good works, were we not in fact propping up the very society that it was now so necessary to transform or destroy? Was it not true that it was the social workers, paid and unpaid, who made it possible for the system to work at all, whereas the real need might be so to undermine the foundations that there was a stop and a re-start? Terrifying nihilism began to appear on my horizon: Jeff Nutall, who had twice travelled in a peace minibus with me and whom I knew well, progressed from his brilliant analysis of the youth culture in his book *Bomb Culture*[15] to a species of disaffiliation in his next book, which made me feel so sick that whenever I sat down at my desk to write to thank him for it, I found I was not able to do so. It was the time of the James Bond 'Cool Cat', which carried an attitude of sick humour combined with dark glasses and the dead-pan look. Disengagement was the key-note. Drug-taking appeared on the scene—most of it arising from curiosity, partnered with an angry desire to flout society.

However, I did not find the right answer within my own age-group, and as I listened to those who had parented this anger and pain and heard their panic-stricken fear, I realized part at least of it came from seeing that some young ones were finding in the hallucinogenics deeper experiences than any of the churches were able now to mediate.

I was helped just then by Theodore Roszak's three books[16] which I read one by one, as they came out. In *Person Planet* he suggests that earth itself at this stage requires an increase in human consciousness. Necessarily there has to be a break-up of the traditional patterns so that the culture-traps in which we are held may be opened.

Certainly the planet *is* threatened in a quite new way, and to be a mother of the first generation in history to be faced with the destruction of the species is a strange and terrible experience.

We watched our three children coming to understand what annihilation actually meant in terms of their own lives, and I only got the feeling for it at all fully in and through their experience. They grew up quite naturally to think in terms of the possibility of humanity moving about in space and visiting other planets. Men landing on the moon meant little to me, except perhaps to arouse my anger (because I wanted the money spent on hungry people, and the moon for me was chaste!)—for them it was a moment of human enlargement that betokened glory! They belonged to a generation which had fallen in love with technology, and one at least of our boys used to say he felt wonderfully fortunate to have been born exactly *now*, with so many exciting scientific discoveries and ventures being made.

My husband meanwhile hid himself from me in his steady attempt to lay the foundations of a new kind of scientific thinking—and from this I was shut out by my non-scientific stupidity. On the other hand, my own inner journeying was mystical, and from this he was precluded by his non-mystical stupidity! This could not be helped, and I now see that nature knew what it was purposing in joining us for a life-time's mutual struggle to understand each other. We were in fact one of many couples engaged in the same adventure of bringing together the scientific and the intuitive in a fresh constellation of human awareness, greater than the usual masculine/feminine encounter.

However, while my husband at every stage was attempting to open himself to the possibilities of inner awareness, subjecting himself to Quaker silence and worrying his intellectual teeth on the spiritual and psychic, my children did not take this path. Truth for them was rooted entirely in the material world, where man had to take full responsibility with the mental and emotional equipment he already had, without recourse to the mysterious. For them it was true that God *is dead.* They were certainly not rooted, as I had been, in the Christian archetypes and could never thereafter tick in the same way. We had had this upbringing and could not find authenticity sufficient in the currency of the old patterns to pass it on to them. Watching their development I conclude that if there is to be a re-arising of the mystical element in man, it will not be from the Christian roots as I have known and loved them. This is why I said earlier that I am aware that my rootedness there is *both* my safety and also *my limitation.* This is not to say that there is no life in those Christians roots, but rather that *as I have known and loved them* in Anglican and Catholic Church Services in childhood, something is passing away that cannot return.

For us all as a family I think the modern equivalent of the medieval *Prayer of Simple Regard* has been in allowing ourselves to understand that the face of evil lies in a whole way of life which allows half the population of the world to live on the verges of starvation, while the other half plunders and

21

pollutes the planet, and continues preparing weapons of global destruction. In this, all the great sins are being compounded into a burning compulsion which seems to make it quite impossible to turn round and act positively.

I had grown up suffering the accusation of us all being 'miserable sinners'. In my teens and earlier twenties I feasted on a diet of fear and self-hate from Ibsen, Strindberg, Dostoevsky, Sartre, Kafka and Camus, with Freud's psychoanalysis underlining the message of incestuous longings, father-hatred and death-wishes. It was with a great sense of release, therefore, in becoming a Marxist that I stopped delving into our evil nature and even discovered I might glory in my body and its strange desires. Later, when I joined Friends I made George Fox's claim to a heritage of inner innocence my own. The new therapies of the human growth movement which I have come to know and respect also descend into these depths within, not to find accusation of evil, but rather to discover existential innocence.

For my children's generation I think the 'God is Dead' ethos has from the outset meant release from most of this feeling of individual guilt. Perhaps it was for this reason they were freed to relate more directly to the authentic contradictions of the world—to war, and people's lack of responsibility for each other and for their world. However, *refusal to accommodate mystery* is a dangerous part of this new view, and the possibilities of technology are therefore not grounded in a human depth that goes beyond reason into spiritual instinct. This causes an increasing split between heart and head, reason and intuition, and morality and instinct.

There is a moment of realization in this alienation, when one ceases to believe in any power that makes for righteousness and the living quality of life, and then being trustworthy, following truth and even selfless loving cease to matter quite so much. The first time you steal or betray there is a sense of contamination—it lessens the second and third time. I have watched this hideous progress in people I love, in a variety of modes, and it spreads like a cancer through society.

Truth is not only factual, it has to do also with the heart. If someone hates me, I begin to know the meaning of hate; if I meet someone unreliable, I taste unreliability. *Freedom turns out to be consciously choosing what one will value and aligning oneself with it*, when it is most difficult.

We become what we do, but we are judged by what we love best. In the nakedness of Finnish sauna it was brought home to me that it is not only on people's faces that what we are is written, but in every cell of our bodies. Meanness and generosity, withdrawal or openheartedness, uncertainty or steadfastness, write themselves in the vehicle which is us, and this we can see in the mirror if we dare to stop and look.

I remember as a teenager, in the run up to the Nazi holocaust, I was once given a ticket by someone on the Underground, to hear Oswald Moseley speak in the Albert Hall. I have never forgotten my horror at the hysteria I found there, the brilliant spotlight on the god-like figure dressed in black, the trumpeting voice calling the masses to a return to the *Herrenvolk* Empire. The semi-trance state of those around me was so far below reason that I could recognize the release of something elemental. I could neither escape from the hall nor in any way let myself go into the passion with which I was surrounded. This, when war came, was for me the picture of what Nazism really meant.

Where there is a spiritual vacuum nature fills it, and the elemental, somewhere along the line, got itself attached to the world of technology, so that we were (indeed still are) wide open to being taken over by the magical and mythic, unlinked to genuine human values.

I too of course was not immune. Certainly during my eight years as a Communist I was moved by a vision of a future time of warm human fellowship when everyone shared and worked not for profit, but for the common good of all. I believed this could be built by means of sensible technology alone. I still believe we need technology, but I understand better that, however excellent the administrative organization, by itself it cannot make us treat each other with fairness, get rid of fear or induce fellowship. There is indeed a gulf fixed between realizing that all the stuff of religion is *Story* (as it is) and realizing that it is only in *the Story* that one can come into possession of a potentiality which makes one fully human and at the same time super-human (*super-human* being not man empowered by technology, *but man empowered by divinity*, his mysterious and only partly known potentiality).

It takes a certain kind of courageous humility to escape from superstition (believing in the absolute truth of the Bible or the divine right of kings or the complete truth of the Catholic Church) into becoming a humanist. The scientific attitude at its best steadily resists the dionysian—the sort of thing I witnessed at the Albert Hall with Oswald Moseley. At the same time it is not by itself the precious everyday humanness which includes coincidence, miracle and mystery. It cannot through factual study discover the substance of the world as creative love. Mystery and myth illuminate things that are factually true, and when they cease to do so certain truths connected with man's place in nature may for the time being disappear from human awareness.

However that may be, the currency of the religious coinage really is *debased*. The gradual encroachment of reason over intuition ever since the Renaissance has undermined our connection with the inner world of the spirit. Thus in searching for the abyss above, we are only too liable to fall into the abyss beneath. In losing our mysteries, rituals and symbols, we become powerless to harness inner and outer, and the inner runs away in absurd fears and a hubris which compulsively brings us to the very verges of destruction. It is of the nature of the case that we cannot imagine how it is that we arrived there!

\*       \*       \*

24

I was forced to listen, carefully and at first hand, to the chaotic prophecies of our folk-soul—through the persons of all the young people I had known during CND days. These young men with their long hair and earrings unknowingly proclaimed the need for the feminine intuition to be developed in the heart of our over-masculinized way of life. The riots of the motorbike boys on 'speed drugs' whom I saw at the seaside in the 60s, echoed American downtown revolt against unemployment and meaninglessness. Then, in the 80s, the broken shopwindows of the Toxteth and London vandals for me were saying something about the way we have been indulging in looting the planet since the beginning of the century. In fact, all this plays out our own inner aggressions, power-manias, frustrations and search for inner identity. No wonder our reply is *more* of the same: more authority, more security, more anger at the prophets, as this echoes the way in which we try to hold down in unconsciousness the pain which they openly act out. Once this was understood, I gained an extended family I did not invite, but which I dared not refuse to own. I explore this further in the chapter on 'Non-violence in a Violent Society'.

Having momentarily escaped personal guilt then, I find I have come back to it through seeing that mostly I go along blindly with the herd (while doing my poor best to resist it—this book is part of the resistance!). I have too many possessions. I quietly pay taxes, knowing that they finance nuclear war. Above all, I fail continuously to follow whole-heartedly the truth as I see it. By too much *inner noise* I get in the habit of refusing to think, feel and act adequately. The struggle is hard and painful, but at least *it makes for life*. I see that in fact I am an integral part of a society which has been crushing down all these messages from within to challenge the machine-made world, trying to hold back the incoming tide instead of accepting it as a means for society's transformation.

Caught between the two poles of over-valuation of

technology and a fresh outburst from the craziest levels of the unconscious, we appear to be heading in the direction of an increasingly totalitarian way of life. As I look back I see that any self-transformation that has come my way has followed a fresh attempt to discover in social action what it really is *to be human*. This is one wing of the New Paradigm. Its other wing is in the discovery 'that in the face of mystery, man is most deeply himself'.[17]

The social action in which I found myself caught up grew out of the Peace Movement of the late 50s and 60s. When the CND movement ground to a halt in East Anglia, I followed my yearning for the taste of respectable life by becoming for six years a County Councillor with a seat in Cambridge City. My Committees were Children, Health and Records and Archives. Because the small foreign community lived in my ward (various nationalities, chiefly Italian with groups from Pakistan, the West Indies and a few Nigerians) I was kept especially busy.

I topped this up by becoming the first woman secretary of our flourishing Council of Churches, a job I was able to undertake because I was at that time an elder of the Society of Friends and thus by a backdoor was accepted in lieu of a 'clerk in holy orders'—which position our constitution demanded of a secretary. It was a particularly fascinating time to be a secretary, as a Good Neighbour Scheme (the Fish Scheme) was underway, encouraging various areas in the city to start up ways of giving and receiving help at street level. This backed up the overworked Social Services and provided a community growth-point. The Council of Churches was certain that in this its role was not itself to start any local scheme, but rather to make known the possibility, encouraging parish or ward-based meetings, where those who lived in an area could see what they wanted to do. This was an enrichment to the neighbourhood and in some places still continues.

I enjoyed this life very much, while always questioning

myself if it was not *too* easy and enjoyable, when there was so much needing to be brought into the limelight which required the painful prodding of society. Thus when a good Quaker friend of mine, looking through my diary to find a free date, grinned and commented: 'Very VIP these days, aren't we—' something resonated and I lay awake over it.

Finally I turned tail and fled. I did not stand again for the County Council when my six years was up. I stopped my connection with the Council of Churches (except for the Social Responsibility group) and instead buried myself in the Cyrene Community, which was starting up work among the vagrant population in the city. Not that I did the hardest part of this work, which was borne by young people who lived in community with the dossers, sleeping in the same slum rooms and receiving the level of money as those on assistance. However, more of that later.

### Exploring Community Living

Down through the years one strand in our lifestyle was keeping an open house. This was easy because we had enough money and a large house and garden, suitable for visitors and campers. As we lived in Cambridge, a wonderful cultural centre, we attracted numerous guests from many countries. For some years, we used always to put an extra dozen potatoes round the joint on a Sunday, so that at Friends Meeting we could invite back visitors. After our trips to America—and my husband frequently attended conferences and did short jobs there—we were sometimes inundated. I remember no less than eleven from Pacific Yearly Meeting lunching on one Sunday, and six stayed on till next day!

During CND times, peace workshops and committees filled up the house—once there were 43 people overnight, and returning from a speaking-tour at midnight, I found three in our double bed and five more around on the bedroom floor! Naturally this was unusual. All the same, most of the time we lived with every one of the six bedrooms full, as we did not believe in having a house that was empty while people did not have a place to live. In particular, there were assistant teachers of languages from the local Girls High School where I was a Governor. These young teachers made friends with our string of au pair girls, and latterly there came Sarah, an Indian nurse from Mauritius, with her eight month old baby, Lyndie. They settled down with us for eight years, becoming ever after an extra daughter and grandchild. This was particularly valuable, as I was involved with the problems of Commonwealth people in the city, as County Council representative on the Commonwealth Friendship Committee.

This open house lifestyle led on to our accommodating a small community during the last three of the twenty-eight years that we spent in the large house in Cambridge. It came about at speed because already we had been thinking along those lines and had come to the conclusion that, now the children had flown, there was nothing special to tie us and we were starting to look around for the right type of community to join. We wanted this to be based in the country and to be spiritually and socially active. At this point, one evening, I went round to lead meditation and have supper with a small community linked both to Catholics and Quakers. When I said we were on the look-out for a community to join ourselves, they seriously asked us to consider if we would not take on their surplus members in our house! I said I would take home the message to my husband and perhaps they would care to come round and discuss it. They arrived next evening (it was early summer) and by the autumn, an extra shower-room having been built, they moved in. Most of the time there were twelve of us, though numbers went up to fifteen and down to ten. At the start we promised to keep the community going anyway for two to three years.

It actually ran for three years and provided us with a life-enhancing experience. Most of the community members were

28

young, and there was a great variety of lifestyle and jobs, including some at university (both undergraduate and research) and technical college, nurses, an occupational therapist, a child psychologist and several unemployed. The older ones included a single mother who came with her two teenage daughters, and a charming middle-aged American who had lost his hearing during an explosion back in the war. Occasionally people came to us from abroad too and we helped them settle in Cambridge. A good many of us came of Quaker stock, though few actually attended Friends Meeting.

For most of the three years we had a weekly House-Meeting where discussion took place as to how things were going. However, when I returned from three months' study at Pendle Hill, a Quaker Centre, near Philadelphia in America, this had lapsed and unfortunately was never again resuscitated. During the first two years there was a half-hour quiet time attended by most of the community members before supper each evening. Supper we took turns to cook in pairs, while other meals people got for themselves, to fit in with work and leisure. Finance was based on the cost of running the house (rates, a repair fund and house bills) divided up according to the amount of space any person occupied. This made it cheap as there was no need for profit. Everyone had their own (or a shared) room, in which they could have their privacy or entertain their friends. I kept on my tiny study and private phone, as I was still engaged in a good deal of public work, and Frederick continued to use his study/workshop. However, he and I slept most of the year in our outside gardenhouse, as we had always done, and by default our indoor bedroom became the community guest-room. For two winters for this reason we did not come indoors to sleep even during the snow.

As a community we did many things together that we could not have done separately. There were, for instance, the amazing evening parties run by Pat, a French artist who was studying to be a nurse in Cambridge. These often topped fifty and went on into the early hours.

At one time a Friend belonging to Pacific Yearly Meeting arrived for a three-month stay, and through her teaching a number of us began seriously to study massage. This especially interested the nurses and a would-be medical student (now a doctor) and opened the way for others among us to start hand-healing. I ran an experimental meditation group weekly, attended by about half the community plus friends from outside, and from this experience I gained courage to offer my seminars on 'The Kingdom Within', which I led at Pendle Hill the following spring.

One of the lasting lessons most of us learnt in the community was discovering how best to eat a diet suitable for a small planet. The community food was largely vegetarian and we had the good fortune to have a member who had learned her cookery in a vegetarian hotel under an Indian specialist. She taught us how to sprout our own beans and lentils, to use brown rice and spaghetti and how profitably to mix grains and beans for the maximum food-value. We baked our own bread and nearly everyone who lived with us acquired this skill and continues to employ it now they have left. Also there was sensitivity as to where food came from and the possibility of exploitation of people who produced it—in places like South Africa and Sri Lanka. Often there were differences of opinion on this which had to be thrashed out.

Certainly the community had its difficult times too. Now that time has elapsed and I look back, these fall into better perspective for me. The chief one of these occurred when we had been running for about a year, and two precious members decided to leave. One of these, under the impetus of a temperature of 102°, managed tó write in the house diary a bitter declaration that to run a community that *was* a community, with someone like myself hogging all the responsibility and taking all the major decisions, without full consultation was quite impossible.

I think after that hard lesson I turned in my tracks and did succeed better, being much more aware how often I unconsciously projected mother-roles which undermined young adults. Certainly we ran fairly happily together after that. Twelve is a good number in that it allows room for some small individual groupings, while at the same time not being so large that these separate off too far from the rest.

However, that penetrating accusation I never forgot. There certainly exists in my shadow-side a bossy mother-devil that I have to resist. This draws the fire of all those young ones (and sometimes older ones too) who have a mother-devil in their background, whom it is necessary for them to resist in order to struggle free and be themselves. I know now much better when this is happening and understand that some of the fury heaped on my head belongs partly elsewhere—perhaps to a mother-devil who cannot yet be faced.

Cambridge is a place where people tend to come and go, and at the end of three years many of our group were necessarily leaving, and it seemed right (community decision!) for us to separate. Frederick and I then decided to move to a small house in a village four miles out of Cambridge.

As I look back I see that in fact authority has to be taken either by the group in a realistic way, or by someone in it who cares. Finally I was so eager *not* to act over-authoritatively that gradually (with the closure of the House Meeting which took place while I was away) the place got really dirty and untidy and the garden even worse. Someone in the house finally said to me very lovingly, 'You know you just slave away and do half the work outdoors and in, and we others do the rest between us. It isn't fair, and I don't think it ought to continue.' Well, we did not continue, but what is beautiful is the number of those who lived with us who still remain very near and dear and will, I think, always be so. When you are in

31

your 50s and 60s, you do not generally acquire such close attachments to those younger than yourselves, and we find them the spice of life.

It is part of the New Paradigm that this should happen. As a society we need to find ways of drawing together old and young, making space which is warm and lifegiving for those leaving home for the first time, as well as those who are at retirement age.

I see now that I have all my life been trying to build up, wherever I go, the nearness of community I found both in my home as a child and also in my Cornish village—where we were so close that if someone died many, besides my mother, would come down to breakfast, saying they had seen the one who died in their dreams and bid them goodbye.

Nowadays I live an altogether quieter life, and my inner life has become more important. I require more time for meditation and being alone, and the fact of my husband's failing health, makes this easy to acquire. Sometimes I even need to enumerate to myself what I *do* do as a remedy for feeling excessively idle. As I look at the list of activities, it does not amount to real laziness. I am secretary to the local nature reserve, and secretary to the management committee of a Quaker home for maladjusted boys. Until recently I worked one morning a week teaching crafts at the mental hospital. I teach a course on Adventures in Inner Space for the University of the Third Age. In the summer I do a little tourist-guiding for the city. I paint, I read, I think, I attend a poetry meeting, a Seekers' group, a women's meeting. I pray with the vicar's wife in the next village. I attend endless Quaker committees. I lead some weekends on non-violence, others on healing and prayer. Sometimes (when I am lucky) I cherish my grandchildren.

I remember the author Henri Nouwen telling a group at Pendle Hill, 'Once I understood that the interruptions are the vocation, I was really getting somewhere'. I agree! The sense of feeling too busy, or not busy at all, is somehow related to this. Unless the outer is balanced by the inner, the activity part becomes a rat-race, and what should be part of a cycle of outgoing and renewal turns into something frenetic and meaningless. New paradigm living is connected with striking this balance and in the realization that there is a balance to strike.

*　　　*　　　*

In this chapter I have mixed outer and inner together up to a point, and there stopped, continuing chiefly with the outer. This is for the reason that there were for me one or two important transformation-crises which enlarged my view of human spiritual potential, and these came as it were in isolation from the everyday, though the everyday had to accommodate them. I want therefore to consider these also in isolation, realizing at the same time that they happened as they did just because of what was happening in the everyday and commonplace.

In a later chapter I shall consider how I came to a faith for the New Paradigm.

# CHAPTER 2

# REDISCOVERY OF THE FEMININE PARADIGM

## Mothers and Children

Boys had a better time of it. As a young child I remember lying on the floor on my back, solemnly kicking the nursery door, eyes closed in concentration. When my mother asked me what I was doing, I explained that I was trying to turn into a boy. Later when I was eight and going to be confirmed in the Church of England I heard that in pagan times at confirmation people took on a new name, and I asked if mine might be 'Ivanhoe'. The Scott novel had just been read aloud to us and I used to spend long minutes being Ivanhoe as I galloped on my rocking horse.

Before I was born my mother, having recently lost a little boy of fifteen months, concentrated her hopes that the child she was carrying might replace him. When I turned out to be a girl she turned away, refusing to feed me at the breast, and I was handed over to a nanny. The nanny's name was Mayhew. I do not remember her, but she became a family legend for the extraordinary amount of love she bestowed on me. But apparently hers was a tiger affection, and she fended off my mother, who she felt was unworthy of me, and in exchange poured out to me the rich funds of her own maternal affection. Being aware of the separation from my mother and its reason was not, I think, the chief cause of my wishing to be a boy. I always felt certain I had chosen to be a boy and been created a girl because of *God willing it—against my will.* For this I was consciously resentful towards God, and my whole childhood and youth carried the tom-boy/blue-stocking mark.

I realize now that I was one of many women then being born

who, from the first, felt an innate longing to fulfil the masculine within. This wrestling for me has continued through life. I needed for many years both to pursue the organizing role—in peacework and politics—and also to find mental structures for my inner striving and growth. It was this last that gave me the deepest satisfaction, and once I realized this, my vocation in public life came to an end.

Nowadays there has arisen a whole generation of girls who know from the beginning that they have a rightful place in the world outside their homes, and who refuse to be shut up under masculine domination. This is as it should be. However, I now see much more clearly that a woman's life spent in serving others and being a mother, just because of its self-sacrificing nature and the necessary discipline of the limitations it imposes, may nurture the inner secret now needed to feed society as a whole. For this reason women are needed with all their special intuitive gifts intact to enter the structures of society in public life, making their way in what is largely a man's world, because only so can the masculine-slanted attitude be permeated by fuller humanity. The danger in this, however, is that the essence of the feminine element in women too may be lost as they act a masculine role. Roles do not necessarily carry genders: it is only as custom builds the cultural picture.

Anyway, I lived a typical woman's life in a typical woman's way. It seems people do not surrender; they are made to surrender. I had to end my revolt and enter the process whereby I became a woman—or remain the crass churl I had been in my teens. However, part of me still remains that crass churl, and this both defends me from exploitation and prevents me from becoming a nicer person.

Masculine awareness as I knew it in my father and as I was drawn to it later in my husband appeared very different from my own. They were earthed into life in a different way. *The world of things belonged to them as the world of feeling belonged to women.* My men talked about things and ideas and never about people. Their objectivity arose from a curious inability to touch what appeared to me to be the essential core of life—except of course in and through women and through the earth itself. They did not read novels or go to the theatre: my father grew rhododendrons from seed and spent all day alone working in this 100-acre garden, while my husband wrestled with huge mathematical concepts of the way the world of nature moves. Again men (priests in church) talked about God, but seldom appeared to encounter Him, though the old man who prepared me for confirmation was an exception to this. I remember we discussed together the status of angels very meaningfully.

I never met a scientist at first hand until I knew my husband, and I fell in love with his difference—his encyclopaedic knowledge, detached sense of justice and the cool clarity of his mind—but *all*, *all*, was at one step removed from reality as I knew it. This I found both comforting (since he was unable to pry into my private thoughts) and at the same time disturbing, because it was impossible to predict just where this odd blindness and deafness might crop up next. In a certain way too he fulfilled for me the human side of my love of nature. There was in him something warm I knew well in dogs, horses, cats, in trees, streams and the earth itself. My father had the same quality. Mating with such a man was mating with the essence of nature.

Later on I met men in whom sensitive awareness was awake: some of these were homosexual, some artists, and a very few were what I came to call to myself *Magi*. These gifted ones acted as bridge-people between the sexes and it has only lately come to me to understand that this *androgyne aspect* is the fullness of maturity in both men and women.

While still being carried away by having fallen in love with my husband's genius, I was sufficiently wide awake, when we decided to marry, to *bargain*. I declared that I did not want

36

children because the mothering lifestyle would take away my essential freedom to be. My husband replied that he desired me as his life-companion whether we had children or no, so the choice must necessarily lie with me. But yes, he himself would love a family, and if we had one, he would, so far as he could, take his share in the chores so that I could keep my freedom.

I repeat—*People do not surrender, they are made to surrender.* Perhaps this is not so much true of 'people' as of 'women'. My surrender lay in coming myself to desire children as a total self-giving to the god which nature demanded of me. Only as a mother did I find the way to go forward into discovery of what is the essence of *a virgin freeness of spirit*, based on maturity.

The job of bringing up four children in fact overthrew any bargaining, because nature itself began to give the orders from within, but certainly my husband faithfully kept his side of the bargain, being as careful to encourage my growing-points as I was of encouraging his. Not all my ventures were successful, however, and when I tried a part-time job during the babyhood of the first two little boys, it had such dire effects on their security that I gave it up. This I did with some inward anger, though when the third boy, and the little girl four years later, turned up, with some sadness I became reconciled and began to spend nearly all my time and imagination in minding them until they went to school. Once I had embarked on it I thoroughly enjoyed this period and wondered how I could have thought it possible to do anything else. However, at eight years old, the boys one by one went off to boarding school. This did not strike either my husband or me as a failure to fulfil parental roles, since this had been the family pattern we ourselves had known. All the same, I did see it as an escape from drudgery and as a possible cure for my husband's severe asthma—which indeed it proved to be, and he had no more over a long lifetime.

Actually we adored the children and though they drove us crazy, this was in a way that made for our enrichment. With four young children close together in age life is a running fight with sanity, but this can produce a creative atmosphere which makes for enterprise of all kinds. Our house though chaotic, was alive; full of animals, snakes, birds, Meccano and engines, clunch to carve, paint, wood and books in every corner. We stayed in our caravan by the sea and on Dartmoor, rode ponies, fished for trout, watched birds, ate fungi, studied number-puzzles, made clothes and gardened. Frederick's fund of amazing stories enlivened the washing-up, tunes poured from him on his piano, and he perpetually surfaced with hidden treasure from the world of science. This, however, was the stuff of his *genie-dom*, and in the commonplace (of schools, lost socks, food-gathering, money, relationships) there were gaps. I remember our eldest son at about ten, when we were due to set off to Cornwall and the car was out of action, suddenly turning to me and saying: 'Daddy just doesn't know what's going on half the time, does he?'

There is a certain sort of knowing what's going on, which for me is the essence of being *human*—something to do with tasting the hidden secrets which seek form and articulation. It has to do with knowing what will be said before words come, interpreting atmosphere and going beyond that into the psychic and spiritual. Of course I knew very well indeed that I was crass (I am still crass), and often while my inner radio brought me news sensitively and correctly, I would tread down these delicate messages under my selfish feet. What is right self-defence and what is being inhuman, only maturity reveals.

At that early time the inner world of my husband was largely one of mathematical discovery, and even in those days he required to spend most of every day alone. Thus the whirl of family life and of work, though he enjoyed it, was hard on him. When he approached old age, the lesson of survival had been learnt, and when family life returned to us at second-hand in the shape of the community that shared our house for three years, he declared this was the best time of his life. Certainly his warmth of heart, cool judgement and complete lack of malevolence, were among the rocks on which the community was built.

The central tragedy of that earlier time was the loss by drowning of our third son, Simon, just before his thirteenth birthday. He demanded to be allowed to canoe from Cambridge down to Ely by himself, taking a tent for the night. It was two days before the start of school, and he hated school. I remember his billy-goat look as he asked if he could go, and my sudden realization that yes, I should let him. And so he went—and without the precaution of any inflatable supports (we did not possess any, as they were not part of our thinking). Somehow he upset the boat and drowned. Looking back, I see that there was something compulsive about this drowning. At eighteen months, staying at Frederick's mother's beautiful house in the New Forest, he gave the grown-ups the slip and was seen running as hard as he could down the slope to the pond. By the time we reached him, he was swimming in the water—and successfully! Another time, at about six years, he nearly drowned while crossing a brook on the Cambridge Sheep's Green, which none of us had realized was out of his depth. We had to hold him upside down and shake the water from his lungs, and it was touch-and-go for a few minutes. All this should perhaps have warned me of his strange and menacing connection with running water, but warned I was not, and the tragedy happened.

I agonized over Simon for a very long time. (Frederick never discussed such things though once much later, away in the French Alps, something happened which caused him to break down and weep, and I believed this was connected with Simon.) The amazing thing was the way in which ordinary family life went on. The children soon began to laugh as before (sometimes stopping suddenly, as though to question whether they might!). **Ordinariness is in fact one's** salvation and kindly. It takes away bitterness and intensity. I was doing a lot of speaking for the Peace Movement and, returning one night after midnight, lost the collie dog in the garden, and he played tag with me for a while. The anger and tiredness released suddenly turned into blind rage at Simon's death and I sat down in the frost and howled aloud. Shep understood the game was over and shoved his nose into my face and scraped with his paw. Hugging him I felt better.

I wonder, as I look back, about the inner knowledge of the esoteric kind, which says that some children who die early are finishing up part of a previous life that has been left incomplete? Was this so with Simon? Why this impulse to water at so very early an age?

I steadily lived with the blame of carelessness with regard to Simon, for many years, until finally and painfully I came to the conclusion that in a family *we are one another's destiny both for good and ill.* We too had parents and they had parents—and parenting is chancy. Try as hard as one can, still one makes nearly fatal mistakes. Love has neither to be smothering nor too aloof. Children, like blotting paper, soak up role-patterns from babyhood. Both man-love and woman-love are needed for fullness, and the chain of life carries on. We as a couple were fortunate in that we both came of a long line of parents who loved each other and loved their children, trying their best for them. In each generation the patterns changed, but love remained. Love is the child's necessity.

Probably my own determination to live as fully as I could arose from seeing my mother's outgoing life. She had abundant energy, produced four children, and organized a large and remote country house. At the same time she became a leader in her part of Cornwall in work connected with women and children. She was the first woman magistrate in her court and later chairman of the Children's Court, and a speaker and organizer on topics connected with women and girls. Having

40

taken a musical training in Paris, she regularly produced the first musical plays our village had ever seen, as well as teaching needlework of fascinating kinds and taking the village girls to camp by the sea. All this was pioneer work in those days and I remember her reiterating to the village: 'Soon you must start doing all these things yourselves, you will not need a squire's wife any more. You young ones are the leaders of the future.'

In fact, plying her organizing skills in what was even more of a man's world than it is today, she did so with charm and courtesy and only occasionally loosed her fierce and over-powering anger to get what she wanted.

At the same time as I grew up watching my mother's dynamics, I understood that this was truly wedded to my father's inturned earthy and contemplative mind. She could be stable because she was rooted in this soil. It certainly seemed to me that women have an easier entrance into the essence of what the world is—*from the inside.* And certainly it was easier to be a man in the exploration of it *from the outside.* The masculine component in both men and women for me carried the coolness needed to approach things and nature, while the feminine carried the whole picture including people.

Looking back now I think that to discover inner truth a certain passivity is needed, an allowing of life to happen without imposing too many reasons and structures upon it. Yet without these the livingness of life can become chaotic and incomprehensible. The world of science and technology now requires to be infiltrated by a new feminine investigative phase, seeking the feeling side of what it is really to be human. To know what it is really to be human is the essential vocation and desire of the feminine side. The tool for this investigative phase is Love, which needs self-giving alongside the right kind of detachment. In every aspect of society we need an increase in humanity. This is more important than efficiency, more important than a feeling of security; it breaks down hierarchy so that this becomes warm and supporting. In the hospital

41

service, the civil service in all its aspects, factories, agriculture, schools, colleges—everywhere, in every place, it is *humanness* that is needed. There should be anger at inhumanity (as when Christ threw the money changers out of the temple), but an anger which flows from warmth of feeling and spontaneity of spirit.

In fact the rhythm of a woman's sexual pattern can provide just the schooling required for this self-giving. We actually do feel different at different phases of the moon. From the moment of impregnation we are no longer quite our own. The initial love-surrender in which we are seized and transformed bind us into nature, at the command of our genes. Both proud and profoundly shocked, we regard nature's indication in our changing shape. Under the indignity of childbirth, the despicable and the holy are merged where our bodies in an animal way take over. Out of this may come the ecstasy of knowing ourselves rooted in nature: 'Words do it, little birds in their nests do it, I'm in love'.* Cats howling in their love-making, great whales monstrously communicating life to each other, all, all, is the same nature that flows in oneself with beautiful and unalterable laws whispering more and more deeply as one manages to listen—and out of this realization, reverence for life itself becomes conscious. How right Tolstoy was when he said that when he first met a new person, the two things he wished to know about them were—first, Do you believe in God? and second, Are you a virgin?

**The Women's Movement and Sexual Liberation**
When I encountered the Women's Movement for the first time, I was in America at the beginning of the 70s, and I hit something which for me seemed bewildering. These hurt and angry women were mostly Quaker, middle-class, intelligent and energetic. Yet they did not stand in the place where I

_____

* A song sung by Eartha Kitt.

42

stood. I had understood and finally come to accept the sacrificial role I had taken on. I saw that *it was life itself* rather than my husband that had had a hand in pushing me into all that had happened. These women, however, blamed their husbands for having persuaded them into a lower status in society, and listening, I was appalled at the arrogant male culture in which they apparently moved. This set of patterns made them feel of little account and undermined their authenticity as people. I sat by and listened as they began to think up bargains to be made with their husbands (bargains I had made before I married). Under my gaze the *Open Marriage*[18] began consciously to be born—but I do not want to spend time in analysing its forward-looking and sensible attitudes here. They have to do with honouring one another's growing-points, recognizing each other's worth and allowing freedom in the ways that one's partner requires it. It points to a unity of spirit based in the modern world, with men and women as partners equal in the enterprise of life.

At the close of these American feminine searchings there emerged to my eyes one unalterable fact, namely, that individuation for both men and women has to arise out of a certain acceptance of *solitude of heart*. There is an inner and secret growing-point from which life flows, and if this is blighted one cannot mature. It is this blighting that makes women say, 'I've given my family everything, and now I am left with nothing'. But a trapped situation is always *also* self-made and arises from self-giving of a wrong kind. Independence is subtle and what looks like imprisonment or slavery is not necessarily to be unfree at all. Lack of freedom lies in something else than prison cells and being owned. No one can *own* another's being. Heart freedom has to be recognized and proclaimed; most of us learn that there is such a thing only when we discover that we are in danger of losing it, and then all life feels like exploitation. But with heart freedom total self-giving and total freedom can exist together.

Perhaps it is inevitable for some women to enter a state of submission, at least for a period. Something in them kneels in obedience to the god of love within their male counterpart, and life lives the woman in a primitive glory of sacrifice. But this swooning surrender must not continue if they are to realize their full potential in maturity.

New visions in connection with sex and marriage were opening up fast as our children grew up. Continuity and connectedness were becoming less precious to society than daring to respond to inner truths of feeling. Sexual relationships, no longer liable to produce unwanted offspring if reasonable care was taken, began to be less subject to social discipline. Expanding egos were now increasingly able to use sex as a tool. In this women rejoiced and also suffered most. Bodies became in a way instruments of relationship. Frigidity began to be seen as the elemental sin in a young woman. Faithful people behaved with good faith, but those still full of youth's uncertainty were now given over to an uncertain society.

In every sphere of life marriage break-up took place on a large scale, with perhaps over half the couples refusing to marry until they wanted a child. For those (like me) with a lifetime investment in marriage-commitment, the scene was alarming. It was hard to see what was beneficial alongside the chaos and pain. As the years have gone by, two things are now plain: first, that women will no longer allow themselves to be regarded as property; second, that there has been a great deal of unnecessary guilt in relation to the needs of sex.

I still watch one-parent families with distress, yet as I watch my own children and grandchildren and other families whom I respect now living freer patterns, I feel there is now a mutual trust and deeper kindliness even when couples part again, than we knew when I was young. The spirit has proved that it has to be allowed to blow where it lists, far more than we dared to imagine in the past.

44

At the same time I know for certain that the human body is the *extraordinary sheath* (or is it *platform*) for another kind of body or bodies of spiritual energies, and for this reason the need to use it with responsible commitment is great. Sex cannot be isolated from our unity of being without a rending division of what we are. This unity has to be won and re-won many times. Nothing except refusal to contemplate it can spare us ethical decision. There will always be conflicts of duty, instinct and love. Our love and sex lives are only as mature as we are and not more so—therefore mistakes and betrayals must happen. Sex heightens moral sensitivity and is a source of illumination in which our place in nature is manifest to us. Life is indeed crude and eternally full of delight and agony. For me situational ethics have to be based *on* something. I find the School of Christ (a path and not a possession) is a possible base for values.

Freedom from mechanism is perhaps the final freedom to which we come. To be free from sexual obsession is a great gain, one without which the contemplative life is impossible. However, it is the loves of our lives that draw us forward into the unknown. The idealistic love of Dante for his Beatrice is as different in kind from common lust as affection is different from 'being in love'.

What I now know and was certainly never taught is that beyond the sexual experience and the experience of a good married love, there is a further one, in which is given a spiritual blessing to the body. While this is not in the least pious it is intensely holy, and when it happened to me, it followed after a long period of sexual abstinence and moral suffering.

This happened on a winter's moonlit night, with a hard white frost. As I stepped outside the door to make my way to the garden-house where I slept with my husband, I heard the wild ecstatic howls of love-making cats. This jerked me out of my pain and I found myself, teeth gritted, exclaiming out

45

loud: 'I demand of Thee the fulfilment of my whole being, I believe in my body and all its manifestations as well as in the purity of the spirit'.

I had not been long in my bed following this, when something strange came upon me—an extraordinary calm of healing bliss began to penetrate me with great physical power; this was spiritual and physical at once, and my body itself began to pray in grunts of joy from a deep plenitude which was an undoing as much as a fulfilment. I remember murmuring: 'I praise Thee with my breasts, I praise Thee with my womb. I praise Thee with my whole self and all my love'. At that moment the rift between me and nature healed at a deeper level than sex had at any time been able to provide.

For me no human companion finally can do more than provide a companion in loneliness. Sex leads on to act out nature's needs, but it does not fulfil the spirit's deeper strivings to go beyond the flesh. Here, another dimension drew me into itself, and out of this suffering and abandonment (because despite the ecstasy there *was* acute suffering)—which was earthy, palpable and quite out of the atmosphere of refined church services or the stillness of Quaker meetings—I understood *the truly holy nature of every living thing interweaving to make one whole.*

This appeasement of body-hunger by the spirit proved to have had the power to renew all my common love (for husband, children, animals and all those with whom I came into contact) so that it led back directly into the everyday world.

Part of this everyday quality meant that I developed a new vocation for working with the sexually hungry and angry, among the people living as vagrants in the streets. Looking back now with more knowledge, I think it is likely that what happened to me would be called, in the Indian tradition, the opening of a *chakra* or spiritual centre situated in the physical.

Soon after this occurrence, I began to learn T'ai Chi

Ch'uan, about which I have written in another chapter.* I believe T'ai Chi increases our unity with the earth. When women practise it, their earth-energies are gradually spiritualized. T'ai Chi is indeed one of the message-bearers of the Yin and Yang culture-pattern which is now beginning increasingly to penetrate Western spirituality. It trains the body in the paths of the spirit and also allows the spirit entrance into what is most vitally its own.

A spiritual blessing of the body takes away the obsession of *being in love* while bringing enrichment to loving. Today, those in monasteries and nunneries are beginning to be very aware of this, and *body language* is seen as making apparent the hidden secrets of the celibate life. Either one eventually discovers oneself 'the bride of Christ' or one ends up a dried-up old maid or bachelor.

If only people understood, as they change sex-partners or marriage-partners, that beyond the fulfilment with another person there is a further one, they might, by renunciation, discover the way to a spiritual opening. This is not a self-chosen asceticism so much as accepting oneself as in the process of transformation. The process is not set off rationally. Life leads into it, taking one unawares—indeed, who would choose to be subject to such agonizing contradiction, biological upset and moral uncertainty! Fulfilment finally comes from within, teaching the lesson in an extraordinary way that there is no need to expect anything from anyone. This does not exclude, however, that at times our growing-point in spirit may be linked with another, who appears in some way to hold the secret of our development. But even in this we realize that we are not beggars in the beggary to which sex may bring us.

When I visited India and Nepal, I saw temples that were decorated with male and female forms practising sexual love

---

* See pp. 71 and 139.

in every possible and impossible pose, their faces alight with calm and ecstatic bliss. This, I was told, was a reminder that all love comes from the divine and in a measure fulfils life's deepest purposing. As the worshipper enters further and further into the temple, the figures become few and more spiritual, until in the inmost court there is an empty space betokening the void from which all life springs.

> So if and when a man or woman moved towards the centre of this being as the pilgrim moved towards the centre of the temple, he will come to leave behind the limited experience of love that is sex, and so, naturally and inevitably, without secret longings, without looking back over his shoulder, since he has lived in and out of the sphere of sexual experience, has fully experienced particular parts of his body; instead it spreads, informs and irradiates the whole of him. The sage in this way fulfils sex as the flower fulfils the root.[19]

Once through this gateway, sex is then seen as part of the marvellous love which interpenetrates all levels of existence from the simplest uniting of atoms and the least conscious copulation of insects, to the most sensitive love of a spiritual man and woman, and the relation between the spirit and God. There is then to be seen the innocent aspect of love:

> The pride of the peacock is the glory of God
> The lust of the goat is the bounty of God
> The wrath of the lion is the wisdom of God
> The nakedness of woman is the work of God.[20]

Certainly in my own life I had to move from a feeling of guilt about sex into knowing its essential innocence, then back again into suffering its contradictions, and only at last did I become aware of the spiritual interplay of sex as rooted lovingly into all existence. Dare I confess that there is also on the spiritual path a crazy quality of God-obsession of the kind so beautifully told in *The Song of Songs*? Something so private, pained, yes, at times so *abject* as never to be spoken? As a young child howls for its mother, a lover for a lost beloved or a dreamer reaching for an ultimate dream, something in us can fall in love with the divine while realizing the enormous gulf eternally fixed between our impurity and the amazing purity of the Beloved. This is a nonsensical plight lodged somewhere in the human psyche which can both suffer it and at the same time know *perfectly well* that there is a fault in the logic and that *we are loved far more than we ourselves can ever love.*

Pornography and concupiscence are real things, and I found it terrifying at times to be seized by primordial energies which overthrew my stability, threatened my commitment and unsteadied my true affection. We really are drawn into a world of glory and terror when we love, and it is very different *to be in love* than *to love.* This is why women in particular so often declare even in these free-loving days: 'It isn't *me* he loves at all' and men, after the first children come, begin to wonder if their spouse ever really loved them or just wanted the children.

However, I did need at one stage to search for the spiritual in and through someone I loved quite separately from any sex-relationship, in the archetypal way of Dante seeking the guidance of the Beatrice spirit to walk into the darkness of the hells and traverse the glories of the heavens. In the East this same path is the path of following the guru, who acts out for the disciple the fullness of his own inner potential. The depth of the disciple's love is given to the guru, and he becomes so tender in that love that the slightest reproof or withdrawal of the guru brings the love into desolation. A wonderful picture of such a relationship is shown in Irina Tweedie's *The Chasm of Fire.*[21] In fact, the guru-discipleship relationship must be one of the most beautiful there is, because by initiation there can be transmission of spiritual awareness.

This spiritual path uses both the natural mechanism of

*falling in love* and also passes beyond it to touch the area of the immortal soul in order to bring it into unity with God. However, I have never known the guru experience in a direct way, only agonized on that lesser thing psychiatrists call *a projection*—which is much the same thing, namely giving into the hands of another wiser than myself such trust that via his strength it becomes possible to reach what is too secret, too beautiful or too painful for me to dare to encounter alone. In this way the Inner Teacher finds voice almost despite myself, giving visions and dreams of a strangeness and authenticity beyond anything my little self achieves, directing me both for life and for death.

## Spirituality and the Feminine

It seems as though the planet is calling upon the feminine aspect of the divine nature to guide us into valuing receptivity and listening attunement to earth's needs. Because of our nurturing and mothering capabilities, women have been exploited. We have also the opportunity to develop the requisite obedience of a purified heart, which can make receptivity and listening conscious. This is our vocation.

A period is now ending where the religious impulse has been isolated off chiefly into individualistic soul-saving tendencies, abandoning the world to wreck itself in technological madness. The danger is that many religious people reacting against this state of affairs are now turning into revolutionaries and social workers, forgetting their special vocation to mediate the inner world of mysticism. Yet is is just this secret and inner life which above all has the possibility of bringing into the light what is needed to redeem the masculine-dominated mind. Women, too, in their attempt to escape from a masculine set of thought-patterns, are failing to express their special feminine genius when they do finally gain a hold in the structures of power. The world thirsts for compassion at every level. In fact, the citadels of the technological society are already being indirectly invaded in strange and beautiful ways by the intuitive and spiritual—as witness Mother Theresa of Calcutta and the gentle women demonstrators of Greenham Common.

Spiritual models for women need to be discovered—and there are few in the West upon which to build. The God-patterns of Christianity, Judaism and Islam are all male—as C. G. Jung saw so clearly, when he expressed his delight in 1950 when Pope Pius XII declared *the Assumption* of the Virgin Mary to be Catholic doctrine. Yet this doctrine still refuses the feminine element a part in the unity of the God-head: Mary is not *God the Mother*, only *the Mother of God* —even if her place is now in heaven.

Early in the Christian era the Feminine was nearly admitted into the divine centre, and one group of Gnostic sources claim to have received a secret tradition from Jesus, through James and Mary Magdalene: 'Members of this group prayed to both the Divine Father and Mother: "From Thee, Father, and through Thee, Mother, the two immortal names, Parents of the divine being, and Thou dweller in heaven, humanity of the mighty name . . .".'[22]

This shows that had Christianity turned out differently and more of the Gnostic churches' material been included, the feminine pattern of divinity might have been established alongside the masculine. One of the Nag Hammadi texts mysteriously entitled 'Thunder, Perfect Mind' offers this extraordinary poem spoken in the voice of the feminine power:

'For I am the first and the last,
I am the honoured one and the scorned one,
I am the whore and the holy one.
I am the wife and the virgin.
I am the barren one, and many are her sons.
I am the silence that is incomprehensible.
I am the utterance of my name'.[23]

In our own tradition St Anselm of Canterbury in the 11th century frequently referred to Jesus as 'our Mother', and in the 14th century, Lady Julian of Norwich was affirming: 'God rejoices that He is our Father, and God rejoices that He is our Mother'.[24] Again St Francis of Assisi, although so afraid of getting tripped up by women, liked to be addressed as *Mother* Francis. In his last sermon preached in the open air in Rome, Pope John Paul I besought his hearers to believe that God was equally *God the Mother* as he was *God the Father.* This indeed is the heart of the new Feminine Paradigm.[25]

Certainly for me the Motherhood of God has broken newly into consciousness. I am aware of it now as never earlier, certainly not in my childhood or middle life. Lately, I gave a meditation on the Motherhood of God theme, in which we imagined we were rocking a baby, then passed on to allowing ourselves to *be* that baby, and finally pictured life itself as a mighty nurturing figure that rocked us. As I led this, the meditation took on its own life and power for me, and with a sense of blissful helplessness I consigned myself to the future experience of death. This whole experience proved life-restoring and rightly led back again into life renewed.

\*     \*     \*

It is likely that the feminine energies empowering the New Paradigm will soon produce their own myths, symbols and rituals. It is by the very nature of myth that it contains the developing secret of a whole society—as the Holy Grail myth was able to do all over Europe in the early Middle Ages.

Myth communicates with the deepest spiritual questions that life addresses to society. As C. G. Jung saw so clearly, when we lose our basic myths as has happened not only in the West, but also largely in the East too, a process is set in motion whereby society is forced by the chaos released to rediscover humanity's relationships with the earth and its divine source, using a new language and symbolism. Inevitably this happens via individuals whose inspiration then seizes the imagination of many seekers who understand for the first time the nature of their deprivation. This is illustrated by the Chinese symbols of the Yang revealing itself in the heart of the Yin, as the point of light in the furthest darkness, a centre of cohesion in the heart of chaos, the feminine and passive infiltrating the masculine clarity and domination.

The historical Christ was a complete person, androgynous, his feminine aspect fully developed and interpenetrating his masculinity.* This is incompletely understood, and I remember some years ago, an uproar when Canon Hugh Montefiore was thought to have asserted that Jesus may have been homosexual—when in fact it was the androgyny of Christ to which he pointed. In the Gospels Jesus said it was necessary that he should go away because otherwise the Holy Spirit, who would lead men into all truth, could not come. Part of this necessity was surely because the feminine could not otherwise be associated with the Cosmic Christ. The androgynous state of mind and spirit makes possible an interfusing of action and contemplation, organization and openness, and a scientific outlook soaked in warm reverence for the web of being which is life on earth.

Many writers have lately suggested that the masculine mind is mainly very *direct*, where the feminine is *diffuse*. The masculine sees a point of entrance for action and makes for it, while the feminine tendency is primarily to see the whole picture. At this moment it is just this *diffuseness*, which naturally sees the whole rather than fastening exclusively on the parts, that is most needed in our rising world-outlook. However, it is the hardest thing for the intellectual and

* C. G. Jung taught that as every man has a recessive female chromosome and hormones, so, too, every man has a group of feminine psychological characteristics which make up a minority element within him. Women likewise have a psychological masculine minority within. The man's feminine side he called the *Anima*, the woman's masculine side the *Animus*.

well-controlled personality to learn to trust the inner voice of the wider spiritual self. The masculine clarity in us all is afraid of the feminine, for the reason that in the unconscious lies the blind world of chaos, as well as spiritual inspiration. It can produce autonomous uprisings far removed from the surface mind, which are painful and threatening to own up to. However, humanity's hidden potential, by which it may surpass itself, lies on the further side of fertile chaos, where what is primitive is allowed space to give nurture to the divine child in us all.

The release of the feminine aspect of the Christ-power is very much related to the body, and by it, the gates of life may open to the sacramental release of divine energies to work in common things. This release is not only magical but deeply natural, though as men burnt witches by the thousands in the Middle Ages, so now the masculine element of rationality is likely to attempt to hold down any mass inner release. However if the natural wave of life which is now arising is fiercely withstood, instead of being helped to do its work of clearing away the blockage of the life-energy then, as the Book of Revelations foretold, it is likely to spread through our civilization as the coming of the Anti-Christ.

C. G. Jung in *Answer to Job*[26] is very persuasive when he says that the Western psyche, after centuries of one-sided clarity based on the figure of Christ, is now suffering the swing of the psychological pendulum, so that primitive, chaotic impulses are taking over the mainstream of being.

For two thousand years, there has been emphasis on the Yang aspects of the Christ, that is on the amazing teacher, healer and master of all spiritual power; He who rebuked the winds and the waves and told his disciples they had only to believe, and mountains could be uprooted and set down in the seas. This over emphasis upon the power aspect of the spirit, has resulted in inflation of the spirit resulting in domination of the planet. But because intuitive reverence has been missing we have unwittingly set about destroying the living and healing processes which actually hold the world together.

The Yin, or feminine aspect of the Christ now awaits our discovery. This is the Christ of the second period in the gospel story. He, who, echoing his mother's *Receptivity* to the divine, in the Garden of Gethsemane prayed 'Nevertheless, not as I will but as Thou wilt'. Just here in the rending of the material, which the cross betokens, a new invasion of spirit into matter occurs. This is the Christ, agonizingly separated from spirit, who by his receptivity makes possible a fresh outflow of impregnation from the divine, right down into the depths of nature and into humanity.

From this facet of Christ, surrendering himself in the experience of darkness, we can learn to listen to the inevitabilities of nature and also of sin, with accepting reverence.

This is neither a crazy nor a strange path. Rather it is the path of intuitive wisdom to be followed in suffering by every man, woman and child. It makes possible the overcoming of alienation from earth and from God, and it is by this means we learn that death is the gateway to rebirth—both individually, and as a culture. Disintegration of being is a necessary gateway to the holy undoing by which we may be remade at depth. There is no other way. This is why Christ *Crucified* is the central symbol of the Christian faith.

This way draws us into the understanding that, as women have to play a sacrificial role in childbearing, so the feminine aspect in humanity as a whole, must now become much more aware of itself as requiring to recognize its receptive role in offering earth a new kind of intuitive reverence. Science has to study more deeply the earth's own methods of working, its modes of expression, its subtle ways of coming alive and allowing to die, and learn no longer to act against nature or think in terms of dominating it.

For myself increasingly the symbol for this is the sacrament of the Mass, taken from its enclosed space on the altars of churches into the wideness of the planet, where we must understand that we eat the Body and Blood of God in our daily bread, either to our destruction or to our salvation.

This is no supplication for a return to the simple life (though for many of us to strive for simplicity turns out to be a lifestyle we need to seek), for without technology, the hungry cannot be fed, nor what is steadily being destroyed now be replenished, conserved and re-oriented. The outer and the inner, which largely have been torn apart, have now consciously to be brought together once again, by quiet infiltration which is the heart of the feminine path.

The receptive and listening aspect of life has now to enter into the world of action—international conference, government department, factory, mine and school. This will only go forward as it happens in ordinary people's lives—at the dinner table (where one wonders whether or not to eat meat), in the kitchen (where a holistic approach to food enters), in the family circle (where there is a new mode of life, bringing together young and very old), in the evening (where the man no longer comes home overworked, while the woman has been alone all day taking care of the young children). The new way stands for peace and against all violence and war; it agonizes over the fact that animals are not allowed to follow their own natures, but are boxed up and injected with hormones. Above all it proclaims that joy and fulfilment arise from reverence for life and from discovering oneself united with all its living processes, whether in life or in the departure of death.

We are ready to hear of this new aspect of the *Receptive Christ*, since it contains the unlived side of modern man, and is his beautiful and threatening counterpart, which demands to be owned, if it is not to erupt arbitrarily as Anti-Christ. In fact Anti-Christ is now to be heard, in the dark rage which is part of feminine anger and male vandalism. If the Yin can be recognized, named and inwardly embraced, then the

56

elemental energy contained in it, will be given power to rise up in creative blessing to unify humanity.

Androgyny as an ideal, is to feel inwardly and come to know the overlapping circles of the Yang and the Yin, the male and female elements within both men and women. We need to produce men who relate to their mysterious feminine and intuitive aspect, and women who while remaining rooted in their receptivity, begin to develop new clarity of purpose. This may lead to a freshly sensitized world of thought, contemplation and action, which is the true meeting place of men and women.

# CHAPTER 3

# NON-VIOLENCE IN A VIOLENT SOCIETY

## Communism and Quakerism

My life has related to violence and non-violence in a series of definite stages. First, I witnessed and took part in *personal violence* in the form of my own rages and those of my mother. I remember her saying to me when I was very young, after some wild tantrum: 'Like me, you have a big inner engine. At the moment this runs away with you and you cannot control it. The same things still happens to me sometimes, but I tell you this is a gift and not something to be woeful about. If you can learn to contain it, then it may be used to do great tasks'. Her own angers escaped into furious outbursts until the end of her life (increasingly in old age when control can be difficult), but certainly she was able to harness her energies in a plenitude of valuable social action.

I too have had to wrestle with these rages and now, late in life, thank goodness, like boxed scorpions (I am a Scorpio) they seldom escape to poison those near me. The last time it happened, someone trod on my sensibilities in the intimate poetry reading of a dear friend, and I leaped up shaking all over, yelled at the offender, dashed out and made for home— and it needed twenty-four hours to return to normal! This is the opposite of right conservation of energy. At the same time I know only too well that I have to find outlets for my anger, otherwise it burns me up.

From personal anger I passed on as a child to realizing that *there was violence incipient in the way we all lived.* This knowledge arose naturally out of my environment—rape was common in the countryside; a murder of passion took place nearby; then there was the 1926 General Strike when I was seven and many shabby and unemployed men made the long walk up to our lonely house in the hope of a meal.

Next in my late teens I saw the twilight areas of London in a two-year experience when I took a secretarial course and worked in my first job. This led to my becoming a Socialist and then a Communist—when I set out actively to resist the imperialist outlook of my feudal background. I see now more clearly how all my natural aggressiveness found outlet in this early zeal. As well as idealism there was crude anger released and a lot of romanticism. In the course of its discharge I found myself part of a surge of disinherited intellectual youth who took hands with an angry trade union movement, in the hope of a saner way of life with the vision of the Russian Revolution as a guiding light.

Looking back on it, I enjoyed the war. I married my Communist husband during the phoney war period, and was lucky not to have him called up, as he had a reserved scientific occupation. We decided to have our children at once, so that I could avoid being called into a factory—thus with our babies, we were happy despite the bombs. While my own mother had no less than forty-one first cousins fighting in the First World War, we did not lost a single close relative or friend between 1939 and 1945. In this war the losses were spread out over the whole population as many town centres were destroyed, but there was not the hideous wiping out of a whole generation of young men which my parents had known.

My comrades and I took the line that imperialist wars were part of the capitalist system, and the extremes of Fascism did not seem to us so very different from what the imperialist powers (including our own) were covertly doing all round the world. In a way, we were right, and in a way, the horrors of the concentration camps and the gas chambers made nonsense of it.

We saw violence in its direct form in the air raids, night after night, going down to the shelter (in Bristol) as the bombers roared over. In fact we were in a basement in Park Street on the night it was flattened and were fortunate to get out alive. It turned out too exciting to be terrifying. More than once we visited London during the Blitz. The Doodle-Bugs were the worst—these, like tiny unmanned aeroplanes, constantly chuddered overhead and then one would hear the engine of one of them cut out and know it would soon land nearby. The rockets, though more dangerous, were not so alarming, as you never heard the one that killed you, because the bang came first, followed by the swish of the descent.

Once we watched a mass attack approaching Filton Aircraft Factory. The whole clear sky was suddenly filled with bombers high overhead. As we dashed underground we could hear the roar of explosions. At one time, too, when towards the end of the war, we lived in the New Forest, we had an ack-ack gun posted at the back gate. One night by mistake this was fired straight along the ground just missing the pub and singeing all the hair off the black retriever that lived there, and several times it went off apparently directly overhead violently shaking the house and windows. The gun half a mile away brought down an enemy plane, and ours just missed an English one (so they said!). Sometimes we used to cook up the gunners' rations in our kitchen to give them a decent dinner, and they shyly presented us with cocoa and prunes for the children in return. When any gunsite moved from nearby, all us villagers raced to the site to search, as soldiers had a way of hiding food-allocations which they had been unable to eat. Some they left specially for us I think.

Finally, when the war was over in Europe, there came Hiroshima. It took us all a very long time indeed to understand just what difference that really made.

## Being a Communist
During the war we had been active Communists and in particular our phone was tapped when we lived in Bristol,

because I organized a campaign for the improvement of the air-raid shelters. These were so badly constructed that some actually fell down by themselves, never mind waiting for a bomb. People were afraid to use them. I also ran the biggest meeting in the country on behalf of Gandhi (then enduring his last term of imprisonment) at the Colston Hall, very shortly before it was bombed. The Communist Harry Pollitt, and Krishna Menon, later India's first Foreign Minister, were among the speakers.

As the war came to an end, the heady fervour which had seized the British working class, showed itself in a large Labour victory in the next election. But this petered out despite the great advances made in social conditions including the coming of the Health Service. The unions lost their idealism, turning sluggish and bitter, and began to resist the de-humanizing of factory life with senseless strikes. The socialist hope turned into an attitude that could see nothing better ahead than a rise in the standard of living; in fact, we sold our souls for a mess of pottage and got the years of 'never had it so good' leading on to automation and a steady looting of the resources of the emergent world. This came to an end when at last some of the poor countries rebelled. The rising of oil prices in 1973 heralded a situation where at least some of them claimed their own riches.

My own investment in the brave new world of Communism had been so great that when all this happened I kept out of politics for a long time, in fact until I joined the Peace Movement and the Labour Party in the 1950s.

Leaving the Communist Party was the end of Stage 2 for me, and I lived in an agonized limbo for a while. It was painful to have cut myself off from Conservative priggery only to discover myself now a Communist prig, who had been blind to the implications of the simplistic nature of my faith. It was as though I had taken my childhood's absolute of heaven and hell and transposed them into a political view. A third of the planet had already gone over to a totalitarian way of life and I saw that I too had fallen into this culture-trap, and only escaped from it at the expense of great suffering of mind. Caught between the two poles of a heartless attitude based on technology and a fresh outburst of emotional irrationalism, I had embraced symbols like the Party, the Handbook and Scientific Truth, not understanding that this could pave the way for an increasingly inhuman and mechanical life-style.

However, as my inner life began once more to flow, I managed to find my way to Quakers and so began Stage 3 in my approach to non-violence. I put off joining the Society of Friends for two years after beginning to attend the meetings for worship, because I could not accept the fullness of the Peace Testimony. The hardest thing was in letting go of the stimulation of righteous anger. I think I feared facing my own anger too and acknowledging responsibility for it.

There had been a hysterical element in my Communism. It was inflating to feel one had *The Truth*, and certainly in my heyday as a Party Member I would have been ready to enforce my faith on others—though it turned out I was unable to lie for the Party. If you feel you are right, then it is more possible to bully others into seeing things as you do, and it was hideous to see Stalinism revealing a totalitarianism if not as bad as Nazism, at least comparable to it.

To be a Friend is to accept an experimental faith. Gandhi summed up for me the whole doctrine of non-violence:

> Truthfulness is even more important than peacefulness. Indeed, *lying is the mother of violence.* A truthful man cannot long remain violent. He will perceive in the course of his research that he has no need to be violent, and he will further discover that so long as there is the slightest trace of violence in him, he will fail to find the truth he is searching.[27]

At the same time, Communism did reveal *an utterly new view* of what freedom is or could be, and it is no use to pretend

62

that Communism is *nothing but* totalitarianism—which is what the West has always attempted to do. The movement of which I was part long ago was certainly not quite befooled; it did have a genuine vision of people cooperating together in the community, without extremes of rich and poor; each giving according to their ability and receiving according to their need. But this vision was seduced by an attempt to find fulfilment in more and more technical achievement instead of seeking it through allowing space for the individual and his soul. 'Small is beautiful' can lead to new kinds of social relationship and creativity in community. People have to associate in networks which include friendly caring. The monster of forms of centralization which make people into cogs in a machine are common to Communism and Capitalism, and the emergent world is caught as in a vice between the two.

The Russians manage to hold down the Folk Soul of the old Holy Russia with the whip of their new scientism, and so find themselves forced blindly to project their inner contradictions onto the capitalist world—which becomes devilish to them. This 'devilishness' is extended to cover all that is intuitive and arises from individuals' relationship with the mysterious. So every outbreak of the instinctive will to self-expression, which is unrelated to the Party point of view, tends to be called 'anti-Communist' or 'a bourgeois tendency'.

We on the other hand in the West, subject to the blind spots of our residual Christian archetypes, have not been encouraged to see the shadow within ourselves (any more than have the Russians) as something inevitably there within, which needs to be redeemed. Evil and good for us have diverged too far, and the Christ of dogmatic tradition is a Saviour image who leads a church militant against the forces of darkness—a sort of supernatural political messiah, who calls us to an 'onward Christian soldiers, marching as to war' approach.

With this background, it has been only too easy to project onto the Communists all that is unfree and anti-human, thus distracting attention from the increasing materialism and inhumanity of a state founded largely on international monopolies which interrelate to maintain huge arms industries. The consequent undercutting of the welfare state, together with inflation, growing unemployment and a disregard of the increasing plight of the Third World can then be understood not as the result of a crazy choice in priorities, but rather as the only way to pay a nuclear arms bill which ensures the safety of a humane way of life. So we have continued 'soldiering on', instead of finding the generosity needed to trust that the life force may finally surface in Russia as fear dies down under the removal of threats of encirclement. In fact both East and West have come psychologically to need the arms race and the enemy, in order to maintain an otherwise untenable way of life.

The American shadow side included also the mechanisms of guilt. The atomic bomb had first been used by them. Paranoia followed—it was not possible ever again to trust an enemy, from now on America had a need to be top. Any balance of power meant America needed more power, or it was not (from her point of view) a balance! Russia on the other hand, having suffered both the 1917 War of Intervention and the invasion of the Nazi War, understood that even the vast armed forces she possessed in Europe, in a nuclear era, were no longer able to prevent invasion. American deterrence for her was understood as American threat. This was borne out by the encirclement of her territory by American bases. The colossal sacrifices Russia then suffered as she became a nuclear power arose from the fact that unlike America, whose economic base had not been injured by the war, she started from a state of poverty. This brought about extremes of authoritarianism against both her own people and those in the *cordon sanitaire* she had established in Eastern Europe.

At present both sides face each other across gulfs of fear and hate which are largely irrational. Reason cannot strike to the root of this psychotic element. The rational approach of humanistic pacifism, which carefully analyses the benefits of disarmament, leaves untouched the deeper causes of war hidden in the psyches of whole peoples. To cry out like children for the ending of war is to remain on the surface. What has to be squarely held in the public eye and faced by us all is that there may well be no future for mankind *at all* unless we can increase trust and moral communion between nations.

## Friends Peace Testimony
It was glimpsing something of these truths that made me a Quaker, and acceptance of the Peace Testimony of Friends caused two streams of non-violence to flow more consciously for me, the one political and the other personal.

The concept of *personal non-violence* was in a way new. I became more aware of the need to tackle my inward shadow. This related to learning how to live patiently with my own husband and children, giving them space, while at the same time managing to retain my own creative energies intact. Because I did not succeed too well in this, twenty years later I found myself repeating the earlier family experience at one remove, when the community shared our home.

I had always been a political type and soon slipped into the Quaker pattern which includes awareness of the issues of peace and war, and so I entered the Peace Movement in the 50s and 60s.

My six years on Friends Peace Committee in the 60s brought me a wealth of experience of the ways peace may be forwarded by individuals. I heard first-hand reports of reconciliation at many levels—from top person activity at the United Nations and among diplomats, to individual search for peace in the backstreets of places like Belfast. In fact Quakers have an extraordinary network of vocation around the world where people give themselves in places of conflict. A Friend takes up a special commitment to reconcile; something which is rooted in the quiet spiritual waiting of the weekly meeting for worship. Quakers went to prison from early days because they stood by the truth as they saw it—and they do so still. I myself, among many, did a minimum prison stay for attempting in a group demonstration to camp on a missile site.

My six years on the Peace Committee in the 60s arose from my active part in the Campaign for Nuclear Disarmament, and this in fact provided the mainspring of my life outside my home. When I lost my place on the Committee, it seemed as though the bottom had fallen out of my world. This loss made it the easier to find a way to slip out of active CND work as well.

For some years, as my children grew into their teens, I was one of the organizers for CND in East Anglia and found myself speaking in little towns around a large area of the country, as many as three times a week, often not returning until the middle of the night. I usually filled in the platform gaps, taking the political, scientific or moral aspect as there was need. The organization for the Aldermaston marches too was considerable, and we often had to arrange for as many as 700 people to do the 50 miles walk to Trafalgar Square. Quakers appeared everywhere in the Peace Movement, and demonstrators slept in our meeting houses as well as on our floors at home. There was, and still is, a warmth of support to anyone in trouble with the law on behalf of peace.

When CND dragged to a halt, its impetus over for the time-being, the immediate cause for this seemed to be that some of our objectives had been gained (as we thought). This widened the division between those who now wanted to go forward into Direct Action (in which there was a strong anarchist element) and those who found the tensions too prolonged. Another undoubted cause which undermined CND was an upsurge of identity-crisis among young people. Certainly it was to do with this element that my own personal struggle to become a non-violent person culminated.

66

## The Beginning of the New Paradigm

The peace movement had demonstrated finally to many sensible young people that however many hundreds of thousands demonstrated, this by itself could never change the whole scenario into something more lifegiving. The blue-prints of the future had not yet been written. The break-out which followed was extraordinary, and in quite a few years since then the whole face of society has changed.

This arose from deep in the folk psyche and everything seemed to escape at once. Mostly it was regressive, but underlying all the dark side something fundamentally positive began to surface. The movement had as its impetus, the realization that we were threatened with the end of everything, and our whole way of life was in jeopardy. My eldest son gave me Kerouac to read as a declaration of how he meant to live. He started university and the Beat Life at the same time, returning home with long hair as the uniform of the new style.

Long hair angered all us parents in the quite unreasoning way that it expressed challenge. It summed up a refusal of all the small family disciplines of years. Outlawry was in the air, nothing could any longer be taken for granted, nothing was sacrosanct and a new set of norms began to be enacted. Sex, honesty, mutual commitment—all fell into doubt, vandalism appeared everywhere, the football fans menace threatened—in fact something monstrous escaped. The other side of the coin was a new kind of freedom in relationship, a questioning of the 'rat race', the rise of the women's movement, and finally the birth of a very different type of peace movement which would offer a holistic approach to life itself.

I for one did not glimpse this positive side in the beginning, but non-violence for me was a determination not to become separated from my sons who were in the heart of the new movement. At the same time every contact between us set our teeth on edge, and there was sleepless pain on both sides. I could be logical about other people's young ones, but in relation to my own I just suffered naked emotion. It was clear that while I must not on any account nag, they required not to kick up against a jelly. They needed to know where we stood. To find the median was the difficulty.

Our parental righteousness fell into doubt and I hesitatingly wondered, as I said earlier, if Marcuse was not correct in saying that we liberals and Quakers had been used as a group, to prop up a society so rotten that any good works were in fact not only useless, but also dangerous. However, as my spiritual life was further educated through contact with Friends, I came to grasp that *being human was an end in itself.*

There had to be illogical, but necessary, give and take on both sides in our family, and at one point I found myself taking a hallucinogenic drug at my pharmacologist son's behest— although I felt this did violence to my inner life. In fact, because I did this, seeing no other way out in the circle of relationships which held me, it provided the necessary experience which enabled me to meet some of the leaders of the drug culture and to have long discussions on differences between the drug and the normal mystical experience. This was a useful preparation when a number of ex-CND activists (many of them Young Friends) sought me out and unloaded their misgivings, sufferings and ecstasies. Alongside the drug culture the new sexual liberation was upon us, and the stress of watching it in relation to my own family caused me turmoil.

By the end of the 60s all this finally produced sufficient solidity in my thinking and feeling for me to begin Stage 4. In 1971 my husband had a three-month job in California. I accompanied him. Invitations arrived from Friends Meetings asking me to speak, and I found myself offering 'Drugs and Mysticism' and 'Changing Patterns in Sex and the Family' as topics. Dates to speak poured in from up and down the West Coast, and the night before I left for America my panic culminated in opening the Bible and asking for instruction. I had never done such a thing before, but my prayers were answered. I cannot remember where I found the passage, but it seemed a direct message—something like 'I have prepared you in a special way and send you as my messenger'.

There were some very deep and penetrating discussions in these California Meetings, bringing together those of parent age and the young; there was a great deal of openness, warmth and mutual acceptance as well as occasional release of anger. Having lived through anger in my own family, any other release of it I found I could now sustain. All this ended with the last Yearly Meeting that Pacific Yearly Meeting held as a united body in Salem, Oregon. Here I was asked to lead the Special Interest Group on Drugs, attended by about 120 people of all ages. It was a deep and tender occasion. I was also closely involved there in discussions on Sex and the re-finding of commitment. In fact, this piece of my life in the non-violent struggle for stability in relationships continued steadily through the 70s when I returned home. It led up to my giving the Swarthmore Lecture in 1977.

But now to backtrack to the middle 60s when CND was slowing down and my vocation there seemed to be ending. I now came to the realization that unless we tried to love our neighbour as ourselves in action, we would increasingly lose all sense of what goodness and truth really were—and this meant politics. Thus in humility I found myself joining the only party to hand which seemed at all possible and became a Labour County Councillor. The six years I spent on the Cambridgeshire County Council were immensely satisfying. During this time, too, I became the first woman secretary of the Council of Churches—and that too was fine. However, after six or seven years of this, I found I had had my fill of respectability and left both Councils and started to involve myself with the Cambridge Cyrene Community.

## Non-Violence in Action

Cyrene had a Night Shelter and two houses, where those who had been sleeping rough could get a bed for the night, and if they were inclined to make the attempt, they were encouraged to try once again to live in a house.

There was a great deal of physical violence and wolfish sexual hunger amongst these men, and unless one had some reclaimed portion of the psyche that answered their need, or at least had a right contact within to these dark energies, one did not succeed well. I was continually astonished at the success of quite untried young men and women in this work, and their power to bear living side by side with drunks and psychotics. Many failed, however, and little wonder in that. To work there was a kill-or-cure experience.

It required the penetrating approach of David Brandon, author of *The Zen of Helping*,[28] to help me understand the underlying reason that I chose to work among the dossers. At our original meeting, after hours of talk, David brusquely demanded of me why I had the cheek to imagine I could do any good at all in Cyrene. 'Do you imagine your middle-class values might be useful to people like this? Or do you get a kick out of it, or what?' I found myself equally spiritedly retorting that maybe it was fortunate for some of them, who now had a warm bed in a bitter winter, that the chip on my shoulder happened to fit with the chip on theirs! We were walking across a wide stretch of green at the time, and he stopped in his tracks and faced me, saying: 'My word! Are you a Quaker?' I nodded, grinning. He replied 'I thought you must be—these well directed aggressions are not uncommon among Quaker women. But I'll tell you another thing—if you are going to retain your spiritual originality you'll find you have to get out of Friends as I have done.

Well, that was a long time ago and I remain a Friend!

David worked with our Cyrene workers' group for quite a while, and I discovered from his sessions that I had reached a

70

point in my life where I had largely overcome my own violence. I was ready to use the energy so gained in ameliorating the violence in society in a direct way. It was no accident then that I had a psychic rapport with the physical violence in the Cyrene houses—so that it became a joke that Damaris had a way of turning up five minutes before any fight!

My daily practice of the Chinese exercises, T'ai Chi Ch'uan, helped. T'ai Chi, while related to the martial arts, is their monastic counterpart, bringing meditation down from the head into the energies of the body. This is the necessary root for discovery of non-violent energy, as an upwelling force in time of need.

The utterly unpredictable event can only play itself out at the subconscious level. One can never prepare for it beforehand except by a discipline of the whole life. T'ai Chi meditation and the Friends meeting for worship are certainly part of that discipline.

Girls are now training themselves in self-defence in England as in America, so that if they are mugged they will know what to do. Personally I believe such self-defence should be spiritual rather than physical. Fear is instinctive and will always overwhelm the fearful person in the moment when danger strikes. It is in the strange defences put up by the instinctual self that safety lies. It is this animal self which has to be linked to the spiritual so that it may function at a higher level. T'ai Chi provides such a training.

I suffered two muggings in connection with Cyrene work. In one of them I was seized unexpectedly with extraordinary violence by a man whom I did not know well, but who I knew had recently spent seven years in prison for assault. When I was attacked, I remember something in me murmured 'You poor bugger' and instead of going tight with panic, I relaxed softly into his violence. His surprised reaction was to stop for a moment to see what had happened, and in that flash my quick Celtic tongue went into action: 'My word, Ron, if you love me that much, let's go and get a chicken and chips . . .!' and at this we both began helplessly to giggle. I gave him a hug and a kiss and he paid for the chicken and chips!

In non-violent resistance I could also be very physical. Once when I was in charge in the Night Shelter, I heard muffled cries in the old bathroom and, rushing in there, discovered two men kicking a figure on the ground. Without a moment's thought I found myself embroiled. I succeeded in getting the assailants off balance so that they fell together in a heap, allowing me the necessary seconds to extricate the under-dog—a young schizophrenic intellectual with whom my husband used to play a weekly game of chess. Together we bolted out through the shelter door into the road, slamming the door behind us.

It took a little while to phone for someone in our community at home to come with a car to fetch our friend, who was bleeding profusely. I then realized that I had left my handbag, motor-cycle helmet and keys behind in the Shelter. My heart did sink a little at the thought of trying to get them, and returning there, the fellows with whom I had had the contretemps now had their own back, shouting to the other Cyrene worker on duty, 'She's too violent to let in—we'll have to keep her out!'

Taking it all round, our non-violence methods failed with the Night Shelter, and it is the failures that stand out rather than the few successes. Time and again, the house had to be shut down because we were unable to handle the situation. When too many heavy gangs were around in town, we were helpless. Lessons learnt under one regime of shelter workers had to be re-learnt under the next. We committee members with accompanying social workers held by Cyrene principles that those who were actually bearing the brunt of living in had finally to take the decisions—even when we disagreed with them. This meant that time and again we stood by and watched young workers allowing into the Shelter proven trouble-makers and bullies. This was not inevitable, as there were in the country at that time some very successful Night Shelters. These were run either by one long-term trained social worker or by people connected with a religious order. Our trouble was too great a turnover in personnel and lack of culture-pattern maintenance.

Certainly the right kind of worker-support and encounter groups make it possible for those who are really as yet unripe to find strength in situations of violence among deprived people. Strength can then be shared and is able to arise out of the fabric of the way the place is run.

I personally feel it is a fact that there is a close relationship between non-resistance and contemplation. Some of the best workers I have met within this field have been people well based in the spiritual life.

One of these was Elizabeth Thompson who became warden of the White Ribbon Hostel in Cambridge when its run-down condition was such that no man would take it on. Elizabeth had spent four years in a convent as her non-violent training. She managed to take in some of the toughest vagrants in town and to contain them safely for months on end. Her loving kindness was combined with a quiet strength of mind that made everyone understand exactly where she stood. You might come in drunk, but if so, you had to disappear up to bed immediately. Rent had to be paid, one week behind and you were out. Fighting was not allowed. Thus, almost single-handed she managed to keep a decent lodging house over some years. Certainly her Irish charm was an asset!

### Training in Non-Violence

Hidden in the body are reserves of peaceful energy by means of which, like human dynamos, we can act non-violently in violent situations. These sources are not tapped without discipline and knowledge. Workshops in inner growth are part of the emergence of the New Paradigm, and to choose the right type at the right time, is important.

73

Lately Joanna Rogers Macy[29] has brought over to England 'workshops on Despair and Personal Power in the Nuclear Age'. This term refers to the psychological and spiritual work of dealing with our knowledge and feelings about the present planetary crisis in ways that release energy and vision for creative response. We need to help each other to unlock paralysing repressions which have given us a sense of isolation and powerlessness. In a strange way, by confronting hidden pain, we find power.

*Massage*, apart from that carried out by trained physio-therapists in a medical connection, is little practised in this country except in 'Massage Parlours', which for most of us have a sexual connotation. However, the radical massage movement is on the move and its American lessons are being learnt. I once did a six week course with Vicki Mogilner in massage (done in the nude), just at the time that there was serious Night Shelter trouble. One night Vicki invited me to be the one on whom she demonstrated, and to my surprise as she proceeded I found myself in floods of tears. She helped by offering me words, first words of anger which I could not use, and then the words 'I care for you'. These wholly possessed me, and I sobbed and moaned them eventually shaking all over with my teeth chattering with shock. She then wrapped me in a blanket and I was left in a corner to recover.

A few days later I had occasion to visit the Shelter around 10.00 in the morning and to my surprise found it open. Inside were a group of the heavy gang, their bottles on the table. They laughed at me and said they had thrown out the workers, and Bobby getting to his feet shouted that now he would throw me out too. I found myself with extreme speed catching him as he rushed, and shaking him as a mother might shake a child, and as I did so I yelled, 'We care for you. We care for you more than you care for yourselves'. Bobby was too sur-prised to hit me. Amid floods of tears I circled the room name by name, mentioning their illnesses and weaknesses, ending up, 'OK then, you don't want the Shelter, and we'll close it down, and then we shall wake up in the night, thinking of you dying in the street!' Someone came and put his arm round me; I got offered cider and tea, and everything calmed down. I said I would have to come back in the morning with the police and seal the house up—and this I did.

Certainly the massage session had been the preparatory exercise for this event. Violence and non-violence are written into the cells of our being.

*Fasting* is certainly not only for Catholics. It is possible to use it in non-violent training. I have a close friend who is active in the Peace Movement, who on several occasions has fasted for the forty days of Lent. He used this method as a means of digging deep within on behalf of his writing and thinking, and also to discover if it is the case that fasting can help one to enter and act from a more spiritual layer of consciousness than that of society's problems of violence. In fact he had a clear answer on the latter point, following a long fast when he went with a group of eleven from Cambridge to the Torness demonstration. This had been planned from the first as a non-violent event. As it proceeded, a group who had attended especially to disrupt, began to act violently, leading others to do so too. Several thousand pounds worth of damage was done in a very few minutes. My friend found a direct summons within himself to stop this, and he approached the police and asked permission to do what he could. They not only gave it, but remarked that they had trusted the demonstrators' guiding group's promise of non-violence, and so their forces were far too few to accomplish anything for themselves. He then called together his Cambridge companions and led them to go up to the demonstrators and ask them to fulfil the design of the protest and stop acting violently. In ten minutes flat the scene became quiet.

I believe the Holy Spirit is there with power waiting to reveal what non-violence is capable of, and by day-to-day practice of it in small and unnoticed ways, the New Paradigm may infiltrate peace into our violent society.

**Recognizing the Violence of our Culture**
There was a long pause for me—and many like me—between the peace activities of the early CND in the 60s and the realization of how serious the world position was becoming in the 80s. I do not think it was really brought home to us all, the degree to which the whole Deterrent Game was a psychotic one until nearly the end of the 70s. To face the end of civilization was for me too big to grasp. It was my children now grown up who brought it home to me. The eldest (who had been to prison for direct action) dropped comments which made me see he was uncertain if he would survive to the point of having a profession and a family. However, by the time the cycle of anti-war activity came round again, I had taken in more surely what it meant, and escaped from the amnesia of the intervening years. I had been helped in this by my term at Pendle Hill, the Quaker Centre for Study and Contemplation near Philadelphia, where I listened to tapes by Martin Luther King, studied Thomas Merton with Parker Palmer and heard one of the Berrigan brothers speak. Peace workers came and went from Pendle Hill, and I was forced to rethink. It was then I think I came to see that ours is *inherently a violent culture.*

As always in my case, Stage 5 in my approach to non-violence came to me in a person-to-person encounter. We were summoned with a small group of his friends to meet Martin Ryle, the astronomer. He shared with us his realization that a nuclear-based power culture was enormously dangerous, even if it was only for peaceful uses. His summons left me sleepless and soon afterwards I phoned an old CND friend, R. W. Hayward, recently retired from a professorship teaching nuclear engineering in Cambridge, to ask advice. In the 60s he had organized a small group (of which I was one) to stand for a week outside the Aldermaston main gate, during the period before the Aldermaston March. I remember we ended this by sending a letter to the Director of the Weapons Research Establishment informing him that among those demonstrating at his gate, were three Cambridge Engineering Department lecturers—all testifying to their abhorrence of the work being done within. The director had been trained at Cambridge—he gave us no reply.

This friend now living at the other end of the country gave me twenty minutes of his time on the phone. I asked him if he thought nuclear power was really as menacing as I had been told. I remember his grunt of hesitation before he began. Yes, it was indeed menacing, but at the same time I had to realize that there were present dangers too; the acid rain and blighting fogs from coal and chemical industries here were affecting forests in Scandinavia. However, taking all-in-all, it was his view that while some nuclear facilities like Harwell were probably safe, due to their very high safety standards, there were others which he had seen for himself which he was sure at some time would fail through human weakness or stupidity. He said he was shocked, too, how both here and in France and America, nuclear power stations were being situated too near centres of population. One melt-down or serious nuclear accident, and he believed that would be the end of the nuclear programmes, because people would become startlingly aware of the high odds, affecting generations yet unborn, with which the industry was juggling.

It was soon after this talk, that the Three Mile Island Power Station in central Pennsylvania nearly had just such a melt-down. This event severely curtailed the nuclear Pressurized Water Reactor plans in the United States because each proposed reactor site produced demonstrations of fear and anger from the local populations. As I write, the PWRs are being offered to Britain, since America rejects them, with Sizewell as the test case for their introduction.

Then Jim Garrison arrived on the scene in Cambridge from

America which for me was a key event. He had been alerted to the dangers of nuclear power via the Silkwood Case on which he had worked as an investigator. It seemed from this that the nuclear energy industry in the USA was willing to go to any length, including murder, to hush up knowledge about the danger factors.

## The Darkness of God

While Jim Garrison was writing his two penetrating books *From Hiroshima to Harrisburg* (1980); and *The Darkness of God: Theology after Hiroshima* (1982)[30] we saw him constantly and thus became more and more involved in studying the underlying causes of war.

Jim's basic question was: 'Why is it that after several thousand million years of evolving life on planet earth, our species—in our generation—has brought this life to the verge of extinction through thermonuclear war?' He believed that we must see Hiroshima as having *humanized the eschaton*; that is, if the termination of the human species is to come, or if the historical process is to be mutated beyond recognition, it is *our* hands that will push the button, and it is *our* wrath which will condemn us to final judgement. Hiroshima is the focal point in our day where God and humanity meet to reveal deeper dimensions within the reality of both. God is in Hiroshima as he is in other events in history; and he calls us through and in the atomic culture to a transformation of consciousness and understanding.

At the time I was talking with Jim, I was also seriously studying Teilhard de Chardin. Jim's book *The Darkness of God* introduced me to process theology—which was digesting the evolutionary outlook into theology. I belonged at that time to a (Quaker) Seekers' Group studying C. G. Jung's book on Job, and it was with excitement that we followed this up with Jim's study which illustrates from Jung's writings the reasons for the rise in man's unconscious dark side during the century, and points out how very similar the Judaeo-Christian view is to Jung's.

Theological tradition tells of God's encounter with man, while Jung explains in psychological terms the way in which this encounter takes place in man's psyche. Man can be seen as a function of God and God as a psychological function of man. God cannot any longer be understood as a Being who revealed the Divine Self once and for all several thousand years ago, but rather is continually moving within us, emerging from the unconscious with an overwhelming and numinous power that appears as Fate. This Fate can be moulded into an image appropriate to us (someone with whom we can cooperate) only if we actively participate in the process of 'holy becoming', into which the unifying symbol from the unconscious seeks to lure us. This unifying has from time to time to be rediscovered. This cannot be discovered by reason, but will arise, God-given, within the hearts and minds of those who seek.

In this country and in this century we have had the bitter experience of what happens when religious symbols become lost and whole nations find the moral mask too stupid to keep up. Then the beast breaks loose and a frenzy of demoralization sweeps over the civilized world. Christianity was accepted as a means of escape from the brutality and unawareness of the Ancient World, but it went to a further extreme than any other world religion in allowing no room for the necessary opposite of man's shadow side. The view of Christ as *Perfect Man*—rather than *He who was made perfect by the things that he suffered*—caused the building-up in the collective psyche of a monstrous shadow (awesomely foreseen in the Book of Revelation), of the Christ Opposite; the Anti-Christ. In effect, this was human evil projected externally and refused integration.

This shadow side for Jim Garrison has a numinous aspect, and should be compared to the God who according to myth required the *atoning death* of his only son on the cross. *Christ crucified* then has to be seen as the central fact of human existence, and the whole of reality should be interpreted through this. *To be 'in Christ' then means to be open to possession by the 'oppositeness' in God that produced the suffering Christ.* The tension we too bear as followers of Christ is part of the tension actually present between the differing aspects of God. But since he is Holy and utterly beyond humanity's understanding, our judgement of good and evil in no way encompasses him, and even intrinsic evil from our point of view leads to the evolution of further creative good. So finally God will be known as he is known in Christ—namely as Love.

Only in the solving of the shattering paradox in the depths of the Judaeo-Christian tradition, with Christ as the giver of life, confronted by Anti-Christ, the taker of life, within the movement of the human psyche, can we find the way to integrate the shadow side. Then we will be able to say with T. S. Eliot:

> And all shall be well and
> All manner of thing shall be well
> When the tongues of flame are in-folded
> Into the crowned knot of fire
> And the fire and the rose are one.[31]

I am left now with a much deeper understanding of evil and good in the Judaeo-Christian tradition. Most Friends do not believe in evil (as a thing in itself, that is, rather than ill uses of good things), but I agree with Jung who categorically stated that evil has as objective a reality as good. If that 'evil something' is traced back to a psychic mutation, which mutilated the soul (known in the myth as 'The Fall'), then that mutilation is as important as our physical reality and will affect it, actually threatening the continuation of human life. We need to take evil seriously and also to understand the marvellous possibilities of the soul's encounter with the divine in co-creating the world.

I believe there is such a thing as a vocation to resist evil in other dimensions of being than the natural, as Christ was said to have descended into hell and loosed the captives there during the three days after his crucifixion. Paul talked of *Principalities and powers of darkness:* I do not completely understand what he meant, but I have glimpsed these and believe in their existence. I think sometimes we function out of hidden inner dimensions of *both* evil and good without knowing it: *Spiritual maturity is to do so knowingly.*

What comes from these dimensions takes body-form (we incarnate them) and the material makes them apparent to some extent. We really are amphibious beings who live in more than one element, and if we are sensitive to this we can act far more consciously than we normally do. Sometimes in a spiritual way we are threatened or assisted without knowing it.


## Society's Crisis of Perception

The centre of our plight is certainly nuclear hazard and nuclear armament. Yet when challenged once again in the early 80s to enter the anti-war movement right on my doorstep, with many people I respected already doing so, I discovered to my surprise that something in me refused to answer the call in any direct way. I both prayed and thought about this condition I was in, wondering if it was old age coming or cowardice. Finally I concluded that I could now see more clearly that if we managed to get the nuclear madness stopped, then without doubt the same power and fear drives in society which made that possible would result in our developing fresh horrors—like nerve gases, biological warfare and so on. *The stop mechanism to prevent mankind from hurtling to destruction is actually not inbuilt*, and when Gandhi wrote that Love always won in the end as history demonstrated—it seems highly probable that he was wrong.

I began to wonder if my powerlessness to go out onto the streets again to demonstrate and to offer myself as an anti-nuke speaker (I do so only occasionally), was part of the general paralytic negativity which has made so many turn away from politics altogether. The giantism of the whole set-up did not seem anymore to be calling out the David and his Sling syndrome—in me anyhow. However, I felt something in me was in waiting and I was involved in society's *crisis of perception*.

Thomas Merton (an enclosed order monk) spoke directly to my condition:

> We are living in the greatest revolution in history, a huge spontaneous upheaval of the entire human race. Not a revolution planned and carried out by any particular party, race or nation, but a deep elemental boiling over of all the inner contradictions that have ever been in man, a revolution of the chaotic forces inside everybody. This is not something we have chosen, nor is it anything we are free to avoid. [32]

If this is really so, then what is required is not so much primarily to organize, as to enter into the citadel of oneself where the alienation from the essence of life can be met and overcome. The need is for *being* rather than *doing*, in the knowledge that action will take care of itself if an energy of goodness, justice and peace is encouraged to flow. This means not so much *being good*—as allowing *good to be in you*—by which I mean the antidote to our false life may be self-generated like the sap rising in the trees in springtime.

At this point the apparent impossibility of preventing global catastrophe in one form or another begins to take on another appearance, as I encounter Something (Someone?) of enormous earth-sustaining power—the Light whose energy feels like *Love*. It is *this* which is certainly the answer, if we find the way to relate to it.

Non-violence is inseparable from the way the planet is put together, but in a sense we have to be very spiritually intelligent indeed to be able in the right way to abandon ourselves so that this Love energy may harness us for the restoration of our largely broken linkage with nature. Something new needs to happen on a world scale so that what is instinctive can be permeated by another component—the spiritual. It is this that is failing to happen, and that is now beginning more and more to show signs of pressing us to become aware of its possibilities.

Because the God-symbols no longer operate properly to open the psychic/spiritual door through which the energies of love can flow, humanity is being deprived of its essential humanness. Unless now we can become much more human and less animal or mechanical, we shall very fast become much less so, because our technology is draining our natural energies and destroying our instincts. Part of this block clearly lies in our inveterate tendency to try *to catch truth in language*, since the linkage is finally instinctual/spiritual and thus beyond man's power to put into words, except symbolically.

Co-partnership with Love energy is needed because unless we open ourselves to it *consciously*, nothing in the new order of awareness is able to break through. It is difficult to turn and look in an opposite direction from the fearful one of threat to the planet, but all the same, this opposite direction is a very *real possibility*. This possibility is now (because it is rooted in nature), step by step pushing us into surrendering our present life-style. This has to be accepted creatively so that when change is forced upon us, it may bring with it a making real of what has previously been only a vague potential realized in a few highly evolved people. This is so, not only for special individuals, but for most of us, so that society begins to have fresh visions of its fulfilment.

83

The beginning for each of us—*is learning to live in the present where power flows in*. This may be a highly practical proceeding. If I go on paying taxes, I must understand that I am paying for nuclear weapons; if I drink coffee or tea, maybe I am conniving at the exploitation of semi-starving labourers. If I eat chicken I must be aware of agro biz and the battery life hens lead. If, If, If, and something in me, at this realization of the need to take responsibility in the everyday, cries out: 'I can't. I daren't. It's all much too difficult'. However, to begin *to wake up* at least involves admitting guilt as part of a guilty culture.

How much all this is due to guilt and how much to cultural conditioning is unclear because one starts where the other ends. Non-violence at least implies *a willingness to be a part of Life's answer*. It turns out too that attempting to live in the present not only brings a feeling of shame, but it seems also *to induce a kind of light-hearted bliss in people* and a new-found ability to touch life's essential livingness. To turn and tackle what one has been evading opens the door to a great many ordinary things too. Living in the present moment implies that we are not separated from the energy flow which is love, truth and life itself—and this is the mainspring of the non-violent approach.

Out of this quality of *presentness* Gandhi produced naive kinds of non-violent resistance which were able to rouse the millions of Indian villagers, weaponless to resist the might of the British Empire. Such ideas as the salt tax, which could include everyone, arose out of Gandhi's own simplicity. At every moment choices have to be made, and there is a choice on the side of being *more* human and a choice of being *less* human and more *automatic*—the choices we make either increase our human quality or decrease it.

All joy arises from a sense of *being*, while the main emphasis in our society is on *having*—with all the technical rape of the world depending on our craze for possession. Locked into the process of making more and more, now that the market has collapsed and there is mass unemployment, we are faced with a moment of truth: we are compelled to ask ourselves—*What is it all for anyway?* Why do we not care for the famine-stricken? Why do we not try to renew the earth?

The ultimate of nonsense centres on the way the productive processes are geared to the world's arms' race (as much as half of all scientists are working for war departments I'm told)— where the goods are never consumed, or if they are, then they consume their consumers!

To live an anaesthetized life is to say: 'This is all too hard for me', and to take the first step of saying: 'Stop! This is stupid!' is by no means useless. In fact it may be the most non-violent and constructive step we are able at that moment to make, especially if it is accompanied by ourselves beginning in small ways to do something constructive—like becoming a vegetarian, saving papers and bottles, or trying to build up a neighbourly spirit where we live.

I remember one of the inspirations back in the 60s, which I felt as I spoke at CND meetings, was to remember the fact that it was the blind obedience of the German people, including many *good* Germans, who thought the top people must be right and allowed the Fuehrer to take the place of their conscience. It was the total lack of belief of many Jews too that the holocaust was a reality, that made them wait quietly at home, until they were fetched for the gas chambers. All totalitarian regimes, as I said earlier, are known by this, that they demand allegiance in place of individual conscience. It is only too easy to slip into the way of refusing to see what is right under our noses.

Certainly our own leaders are not psychotic maniacs like Hitler. All the same, the whole situation of trying to defend ourselves from the Russians (and the Russians trying to defend themselves from us) by means of weapons that would obliterate both, is *psychotic madness*. Unless we manage to speak out, we are as much to blame as those who wondered where the trains loaded with Jewish families were being taken—and dared not press their enquiries. The gas chambers could only work because factories produced parts for them, the railways ran, the storm troopers trooped and ordinary neighbours as a whole said not a word, nor did the churches, nor did the legal system, nor did the philosophers and universities, nor did the scientists. The few that spoke out died too.

The nuclear holocaust can only happen because we ask too few questions. But now the questions are on TV, in the newspapers, being asked in mass demonstrations, by the trades unions and Labour Party, and in the churches—and we can only escape them by blocking our ears or turning off the switch. The first step is to begin really to listen; the second step will reveal itself in an individual way to each person. After listening, usually action is not far behind.

And the price? The price is daring to unblock the energy channels through which flows the ability to live in the joy and terror of the present moment. *This is a world transformation crisis, and we cannot escape it.*

We are being called creatively to add new values to the world; values about what it is to be human—to be a man or a woman or a child. The non-violent life helps the growth point within each of us to remain inviolate. An illustration is the way a small plant may push up its shoot through a crack in a hard pavement; frost and rain help—and it just keeps on seeking the light with life empowering it, until the pavement gives way. Enormous energy of life is on the side of the emergence of man's higher potential and this may be known as courage, joy, peace, truth and love.

So now it seems that after all I am back where I was in the 60s with a message I want to shout from the housetops—Life is on the move and a holistic approach to it will bring the answers that heal our society and reunite us to mend our damaged and afflicted planet.

# CHAPTER 4

# A HOLISTIC APPROACH TO HEALTH

## The Holistic Health Movement

In the early 70s I started to give talks on *A Healthy Approach to Body, Mind and Spirit.* The essence of my message was the discovery that to be healthy, we need to learn how to summon up our inner resources by bringing them into contact with the rhythms of nature. These rhythms sometimes change tempo within, and we have our winters and summers, times of rest and times of outgoing activity. We must learn to listen to their flow.

I had come to see my body as the outermost sheath of two subtler bodies, the psychic and the spiritual. With the psychic one sometimes experiences telepathy and extra-sensory perception, while the spiritual is the inner growth-point connected with the Light within. Only if one is reasonably well integrated in these three together is good health likely to be maintained. This agrees with William Blake's view that man has no body distinct from his soul—which signifies that we *are* our bodies and thus have to take responsibility for their manifestations.

I realized too that we are held within a process of world and social evolution, so that health has to be seen in a much wider context than the purely medical. The process of creation and dissolution present everywhere in the world happens in us too. Along with this I increasingly discovered the inner powers for healing—and even found myself involved in giving and receiving charismatic healing.

With attitudes like this it was inevitable that I began to meet people of like mind—until now, in the 80s, I understand that what was previously only small groups has turned into the Holistic Health Movement.

This movement is about the process of self-renewal. It is founded on seeing illness and health in a wider context than before and is not so much an emerging hospital—and university-centred affair as a spreading network which gradually includes more and more people, who now want to study how best to be well.

Much of this is in no way antagonistic to traditional medicine, but it does emphasize full cooperation between doctor and patient in the healing process and invites an attempt at a life-style which is more in line with natural processes. It encourages us to listen to what our bodies are trying to say when they become ill, and to attune to the possibility of body, mind and spirit interrelating in a more comprehensive way.


**Health**

Individual health relates to the way we live—and our society is in many ways a sick one. We are undermined by largely unacknowledged fears (nuclear hazard, fear of death). Unemployment and job-competition affect many lives. Keeping up with the Joneses is a constant pressure for some. We eat a great deal of junk-food, live at inhuman speed, suffer constantly from over-stimulation, our atmosphere is often polluted and it is customary to be under-exercised. Many lives are lonely and without loving human contact. Our society does not prize enough the interweaving of people to make up human warmth and value.

This being so, any single person's disorder has to be seen against the background of a general malaise, and inevitably it is the delicate and sensitive who will tend to suffer most. For this reason we must not necessarily blame ourselves for becoming ill, but at the same time we do need increasingly to try to take responsibility for health and learn how best to resist the pressures that society lays on us. People are cells in a web of relationships, and all the time we are both giving and receiving good and bad energies. There is need for *the conservation of one's own energy* as much as for conservation of energy in the world's productive processes. There are those who tend to build up reserves of vitality and those who perpetually squander both their own and other people's too.

At the moment there is a gradual lowering of standards in the health services, partly because more and more people expect high technology treatment. At the same time, many of us are beginning to understand more clearly that we want medical people not only to be scientists, but also wise human beings able to advise and comfort. This implies a health service where organization is slanted to produce the needed counsellors to help doctors, who have too many people passing through their consulting rooms. To be over-pressed causes the doctor to direct his attention chiefly to the bodily machine rather than the person. Even a short while ago there was little in the modern physicians' training which related to psychosomatic medicine, and it is chiefly for this reason that the *complementary medicine movement* has been on the increase. It is indicative of the change in public attitude that the phrase now in current usage is changing from *fringe* to *complementary* medicine.

In fact the heavily laden health service, with all its elaborate and expensive equipment, cannot proceed much further in its present direction, if only because society is not able to afford to pay for it. This fact helps on the vision that a simpler and less expensive need is to cultivate healthier and more natural approaches to being born, living, growing old and dying.

In fact the interplay between traditional and complementary medicine is progressing fast—if news of it in the mass media is any indication. Just in the past year I have seen television programmes on any number of the new approaches to health. These included:

the use of hypnotism—both for traumas and in dentistry; a gentle way with cancer;

spiritual healing practices of several kinds;

hospices for the dying, where tender loving care and spiritual and mental preparation for death are the declared aims.

For many years now osteopathy has worked alongside traditional physiotherapy and is now being recognized widely as sometimes able to help where traditional methods fail. Acupuncture, herbal treatments, colour healing, homœopathy, polarity therapy and many other forms of healing are becoming well known, while the National Register of Charismatic Healers includes hundreds of names.

On the mental health side, both in mental hospitals and very broadly outside them, there is a growing movement by means of which the expensive one-to-one therapy of the psychiatrist's couch is replaced by group settings, where people with reasonable expertise can help each other. Dream study, Transactional Analysis, Gestalt therapy, Psychosynthesis and many other kinds of encounter at depth, some better, some worse, bring people together to assist each other in reconnecting with the flow of life.

In the heart of society itself too there has been a flowering of organizations which join together those in trouble. Alcoholics Anonymous was one of the pioneers, and now there is Cruse for widows and widowers, Gingerbread for the single parent, Samaritans for those in despair, Linkline and Friend for homosexuals. Of another kind are the societies supporting those who are ill, like Mind (for the mentally ill and their relatives), Age Concern for the old, Cancer Help and a great many more. Neighbourhood schemes back up the social services and volunteer schemes help out in hospitals. In fact anyone with initiative may find a niche in which to give and to receive when they are themselves in need.

All this is the growing point of the New Age Paradigm in

building healthier ways of life, because it draws people together to take responsibility for one another and for themselves. For me, all this has been a great source of enrichment both through the people I meet in connection with it and also because the ideas flowing from there have infiltrated my own thinking on every level connected with health.

## Life as a School of Being

Society has lost its intuitive knowledge of the psychic and spiritual and is very largely based in the material alone. Even the instinctive belief in life after death, held by every other civilization until now, is disappearing. For this reason there is bound to be psychosomatic disorder and distress. However, some of this alienation may be part of the evolutionary drive which, rightly accepted, will encourage development in man's spiritual and psychic component.

If nature, on the move, forces us into a revolution in lifestyle in a physical way (because we cannot continue to use up the good things of the earth at this rate), then inevitably we shall be caught off-balance in the way we experience. Darkness and pain are the result and they are the only mode by which basic change can come. However as Blake wrote in his 'Auguries of Innocence':

Joy and Woe are Woven fine
  A clothing for the soul divine
Under every grief and pine
  Runs a joy with silken twine.
Man was made for joy and woe;
  And when this we rightly know,
Safely through the world we go.

To understand what is happening helps alter what is *a crisis* into a *transformation crisis* and links individuals in a redemptive way to the *transformation crisis of the world.* To be so linked makes it possible to take suffering as a necessary corrosive to unblock the free-flowing rhythms of life. Trouble can detoxify, in the sense that it halts fantasy, unnecessary planning ahead and confronts us with the present moment.

As the best healers always enquire about a patient's way of life, so to be in health I have to understand what my life really consists of and from time to time ask myself *whether I am living the kind of life I most want to lead.*

This question usually arises when I find myself embedded in a network of relationships and work, into which I entered willingly, but which now hems me in. In fact my home, work and religious commitments, are both the supportive structure of my life and at the same time its cross. In order to mature (because I become what I do) I have to find ways both to be quite faithful to any serious commitments and also to follow what is life-giving, by resisting what is no longer *for me.* If I baulk at resolving a particular form of constriction or contradiction constructively, either taking the line of least resistance or brashly destroying my relationships, then I notice that something of a similar sort recurs until finally I act authentically. Since I noticed this, I have begun to see the same pattern in others' lives too, and it has made more real the idea of *life as a school of being.*

I can only love my neighbour *as* myself and never more so, because if I try to be too self-giving without completing the circle of receiving back so that I can be renewed, things begin to go wrong and in extremes my body has a way of finding an escape-mechanism through falling ill.

I heard an apocryphal story lately, of a busy vicar who slipped on a banana skin and found himself in hospital. He complained to his guardian angel and the reply came: 'Oh no indeed, this was no mistake! I carefully laid it in your path—as the only way to halt your stupid overwork!'

In the same way that sex-signalling is perpetually taking place (women signalling readiness to men, and men signalling readiness to women), so also nurturing-signalling, intellectual-signalling, anger-signalling, profit-making signalling and so on are taking place. The outside world appears to inter-relate with me all the time. If I act constructively I tend to receive positive feedback, if negatively then I receive negative feedback. This often extends into matters over which I have no control whatever, and I have come therefore to think that I need to take responsibility for understanding *just what I am actually signalling and should send a blessing ahead of me into the substance of everything that I do* because my deepest desires are reflected in what happens to me.

Consciously I now need to grasp the fact that there is an underlying unity to all life. Life is perpetually signalling to me, *because I am the microcosm of the macrocosm.* As I understand the teaching of modern biology, each cell bears the pattern of the whole in miniature like a hologram—and so in greater degree do I. Spiritually (as well as physically and mentally) I can view myself as a cell in the being of God. As the cells in my body (if they are not cancerous) obey the 'will' of the whole and make for wholeness, so my conscious awareness has to learn the way of obedience to the divine will. The evolutionary venture into consciousness has momentarily jeopardized the unity of creation. Only by the further step of consciously uniting myself again (instinct giving way to its deeper form which is the spiritual intuition) can my desire to reknit to the unity of creation be brought about. Incidentally, while I have always stood aside from astrology and the I-Ching (the Chinese ancient Wisdom Book which impressed C. G. Jung so much) while from time to time allowing practitioners of these skills to give me a reading—each time I have received extraordinary inward help. If all life from furthest to nearest is actually related (as I now know them to be), this might very well be genuine, as ancient tradition understood and increasing numbers of very reasonable and well adjusted people still believe.

93

All life from highest to lowest then is a school of being gradually arising from non-being, and it is possible to signal blessing ahead into the substance of material things and for this to have actual effect on the material plane. This I do in my early morning quiet hour when I glance ahead at what my day is likely to bring, the people with whom I shall come into contact, the cake I shall bake, the grass I shall mow—and so on. If I am going on a journey (and I am a neurotic traveller) I can take particular care to ask a blessing on everything connected with it.

The body works better when it receives cheering rather than gloomy signalling. It is now generally accepted that certain diseases may relate to mental conditions: ulcers and hypertension can arise from business men's pressured living; heart trouble goes with overstrain; arthritis with inability to relax; cancer with shock, bereavement and unfulfilled basic desire, as well as identifying with the world's contradictions— and so on. However, it is a simplification to think that these are the *only* causes.

After all, *life is for living* and sometimes I gladly enter into situations which use up my inner resources. Cavers exploring deep underwater tunnels and caverns find that in dangerous situations they use up far more air in their oxygen cylinders than normal—in the same way when under strain I produce body patterns which cannot long be sustained healthily.

Life invites me to commit myself to it whole-heartedly. If I refuse, then I shall feel meaningless. *Give and it shall be given unto you* is also a rule of health. Self-renewal comes from completing the circle of giving and receiving. There is a greed which wants always to be the Giver, but unless I can receive back from the essence of the life-flow, my power to give will remain very limited.

This is why consideration of my life-style and the question *Am I living the life I really want to lead?* is primary. I tend towards manic and depressive addictions and unless I can get these out into the open I am stunted by them. Often what appeared in the past to hem me in was governed by these small addictions inbuilt to the pattern of my life. Habits are necessary, addictions are not! People only think of addiction in terms of drugs and alcohol—but it can be anything, like possession of unnecessary kitchen equipment, being too house-proud, watching television or always wanting company. I can even be addicted to meditation and spiritual search, to the exclusion of tying it up to the present moment and its demands. Addiction can be recognized because it is an escape instead of going forward into engagement; it is a one-sided search that leads to separation from wholeness. Not that a specialization is not needed at times—it is, and not only genius but all spiritual search at depth is based on it. What is necessary, though, is to find the golden mean, combing out what is superfluous in order to make room for what is most essential.

There are times in every life (and certainly in mine) when one feels forcibly shut in and prevented from living fully. At the moment I have a friend (who used to be an enclosed order sister) whose entire energies are now taken up with her four-year-old and her one-year-old twins. There is practically no time, either day or night, when her family are not making demands on her and any quietness comes as a gift! As I watch her in her serene and gentle mothering, I think back to when I was in like case with three young boys under five. There were times when I was much more akin to the furious young parent of whom I heard recently who said: 'Me! I live in a state of perpetual rage!' Fortunately this was not commonly the case, though I think I over-stimulated everyone in my vicinity. It is this state of anger and over-stimulation which is the heart of the violent society. Non-violence is learning not only how to assuage one's animal rage, but also how to live gently, peacefully. There is indeed a narrow dividing line between living selfishly and loving your family *as* yourself. One pointer is to know that unless the creative flow of vitality is kept going, it is impossible to give adequately, and health depends upon that kind of self-renewal.

I remember the time when I first instituted 'Mother's quiet time'. There was family resentment and I had feelings of trepidation and guilt. No, I would *not* come to the door, I would *not* settle a quarrel, I would *not* answer the phone, I *was* going to be all by myself without interruption! This started with a meagre half an hour and finally stretched into a much longer period, becoming an important ingredient in my lifestyle. It seemed to make the whole ensuing day more relaxed and less under pressure of feeling hyper-active.

The body takes the rap for sick emotions (jealousy, hate, downright misery, bitterness, love-craving) and for departures from the deeper rhythms of existence (like living too fast). However, 'madness is to genius oft allied' is not nonsense. Our unavoidable times of tension can be extraordinarily productive of maturity, and there may be outpourings from the unconscious which, though they bring us to the abyss of being, yet fulfil all that our lives have been travelling hopefully towards for a long time before.

I discovered this in particular when I was both carrying heavy responsibilities and at the same time needed to pursue the inner life with ardour. This resulted in the everyday often taking on a visionary aspect. While I was deeply moved by this, I knew very well that it was due to overstrain, and while being quite enamoured of the state I guessed I would go crazy if it continued! What it did lead to, however, was the realization that it was towards this kind of inner seeing that my desire was guiding me, and I hoped that a time might come when I should be able to experience more deeply without the accompanying stress. Now, much later in life, I realize that I do indeed observe the world more penetratingly in a natural way. My connection with people, animals, plants and scenery is more vital, my sense having been to some extent refined spiritually. There is still, however, for me an alienation, a lovelessness, which I cannot break down for myself, but which I pray life may at some time find a way to break down for me.

Prayer and meditation in particular are ways which make possible the return to the inner space which is the living source of health and healing. The more hyperactive anyone is, the more he or she requires to return to inner renewal. Children and animals by dint of their natural state live in the present moment, and so find self-renewal easily. It is the alienation from this source that breeds a feeling of insecurity and alienation which takes many forms and results in a sick society.

Some relationships feed and succour; others drain. To be forced to remain with someone who perpetually sucks at one's vitality can even be death-dealing. To be conscious of energy-depletion is the first step. The next (if escape is impossible) is to discover power to resist. I have listened fascinated to Pir Vilayat explaining the use of mantras to increase inner power, which can be used—for instance, by a very junior member of a firm who is perpetually being bullied by someone in a higher position! Prayer is a source of inner strength and renewal and it has its individual self-taught rules for those who practise it. However, it is really true that God's strength may be made perfect in weakness.

### Life's Inner Stages

If life is a school of being, certainly it has stages. Fulfilment comes from seeing these as a part of a single creative process from birth to fulfilment, from fulfilment to decline and death. What looks like decline outwardly may in fact be a leaving behind of what is finally inessential.

I suppose a satisfactory lifelong relationship is one in which there is a mutual exchange of natural, mental and spiritual energies, and when this comes to an end with the death of one of the partners, it really does take not less than three years for the remaining person to discover **how to renew** vitality in the everyday.

Bereavement then can either *break us down* or *break us open* to receive increased life. When it happens, there is a sense in which we are helpless to help ourselves, and only a patient and steady desire for renewal of life can open the way. Often the remaining partner just desires death. The condition of waiting is perhaps the beginning of the final surrender needed when we die. This has to be seen not as 'giving up', but as giving up one sort of life for *a higher.* We only understand this release as we allow life to have its way with us. The word *Health* comes from *Holy*, and the healthiness of the divine flow is there insofar as we find the way to surrender to it.

In managing increasingly to open to the forces of life (which I personally see as *the Divine Beloved*) there spontaneously arises a prayer that one may hear the summons to depart when one's time comes—so that the body's undoing may be known as an inrush of love-energy which bears one into the fullness of the Light. The mystics say that *Death is like Ecstasy*, and to overcome the fear of self-surrender in prayer is a preparation for it.

The travail of birth is a picture of the travail of death. If death is viewed as a means of uniting with the essence of life, then surely it becomes possible to accept it readily not only for oneself, but (what is harder) on behalf of those one loves and appears to lose.

As children, if we have been happy, we are not too early separated from wholeness. I am told that young children who have been well loved generally die without much fear. At some point, though, we have to confront the fact that all is transient. Death will carry away all we love best. But there has to be a reaching beyond death which happens by means of an inward surrender in hope and faith. If I invite life and embrace it, then life appears to understand this and gives itself to me, and in so doing it separates me more and more from the false ego-kit picture I perpetually maintain as to what I am. This whole process I describe to myself in the Christian archetypes of the cross and resurrection.

Passing through life's stages brings growth and maturity along with joy and pain. Being a teenager is both delicious and agonizing. One scarcely knows what one is; sometimes quite grown-up and the next a mere child; ready at one moment to challenge one's entire background and its values, and in the next only too ready to receive help and succour from it; at times identifying with one's family and at others striving to be separate.

In those struggles all the future struggles of life are pre-figured. There is a real need to succeed in these heroic small attempts to be oneself, for if one fails then it is a gateway to a life of failure. As I look back, it was my adolescent adventuring which was the hardest and least endurable of my whole lifetime, because I had no sense of security about where I was going. I think our children found the same; perhaps we all repeat these patterns.

The alarming moment of realization that the tide of life is bearing everything away came to me in my thirties. I remember losing all assurance that there is meaning in anything and chewing on that bitter thing day and night. I think it was the near death of one of our little boys when he was two that brought this home to me first. In some sense this was much more agonizing than when one of them actually was drowned, a few years later, because by then I had better come to terms with death. At the earlier time I felt a sense of purposelessness of all effort of every kind in the light of universal transience. In Dostoevsky's novels, one discovers which of his characters believe in God—because the atheists all commit suicide. This I understood very well, because at that time I had no belief.

In the death of our son I knew a heavy sense of guilt, of having failed. It seemed to me that my failure was part of a failure that went deep into the roots of all life, so that one could not escape it. It was as though death was the ultimate seal on my failure. From then on I began to work hard on the subject of death. This took the form of a question: 'What is Death?' This (like a love affair!) was always around on the periphery of my mind. While I did not become obsessed with it or lie awake on it (much anyway), I did not stop until finally it was revealed to me that *death is a mystery* rather than just a hole—and a fertile one at that. During this time I sometimes cursed myself as superstitious and fearful, guessing I was demanding a return to my childhood's sense of security. Looking back, I see I was unable to make conscious *what I really knew.* This contradiction left room for me to accept without question my dead father's psychic return to visit me, without taking this to be any kind of proof of life after death. I think this was because I saw it as *merely psychic*, and at that time my mind was demanding scientific evidence.

It is very easy in fact to compartmentalize in that way, discounting evidence, however powerful, that comes from one's inner world, because it does not fit in with one's structures of thought. A great many *peculiar things* can happen which we simply relegate to forgetfulness because of tight attitudes which cannot accommodate them. Insight comes from listening both to outward and material evidence and *also* to inward evidence. Health is based on an ability to align these sorts of knowledge so that they interrelate and bring enrichment of understanding.

### Self-Healing and Healing Gifts

The area of the New Paradigm in Health that has always most concerned me has been that of charismatic healing and the increasing discovery of the ability to live in a state where the body is assisted to heal itself.

From early times healing has been related to the inner life: the shaman, the saint and Christ himself treated ill people spiritually and brought them back to health. Every village had its wise women and herbal healers. Nowadays in England the directory of charismatic healers demonstrates first that there are a great many of them and secondly that their work is now out in the open and being accepted by society in a fresh way. Anyone who desires such a healer's help is likely to be able to find one. I and my friends give and receive healing as part of a way of life, as nothing unusual, and this goes alongside using the offices of traditional doctors.

The healing gifts appear to be common to us all, and I personally know from experience that 'where two or three are gathered together' seeking spiritual help, healing begins to flow. Even those without much natural healing ability (like myself) find that sometimes we heal, and our power to do so increases tremendously in a spiritually centred group. There has been a great deal of recent study on the subject of healing and it is now possible scientifically to observe vibrations issuing from healers' hands. Again there seems to be different kinds of healing, some 'magnetic'* and some that I think of as Holy Spirit healing. It is this last in which I am involved in my work with groups.

I have been fortunate in my healing experience to have had a connection as a Quaker with the Friends' Fellowship of Healing for over twenty years. This has provided a solid foundation for exploration of many types of healing, while at the same time attending a regular prayer group based on silence, in which the names are spoken of those for whom a blessing is asked. The practice does not dwell on the sickness or distress of the person, but rather on the idea of their wholeness. Those who attend the group open themselves as channels for the Holy Spirit. This in no way intrudes upon the one prayed for, but rather should act as a catalyst to help the inner capacities for healing and wholeness. Many Quaker

* The word *magnetic* is put in quotation marks because it is a vibration which has not yet been explored: it is not magnetism in the scientific sense.

meetings have such Friends' Fellowship of Healing groups alongside the meeting for worship, and these provide a centre for those in need to ask for help—as well as a school of quiet prayer for those who attend it. The healing gift increases with use and those setting out along the path of prayer for others, of hand healing and absent healing, are helped by working with those further along the way. The central lesson to be learnt is that the blessing and healing has nothing to do with us, but rather flows in from beyond. For this reason there is no need to feel particularly special oneself when it happens. Inflation is so very easy if this is not clearly known to be the case. For this reason to have prayer partners is in many ways salutary.

For beginners, I think to heal at a distance is much more difficult than giving it to someone directly in the room with the laying-on of hands. It is becoming more common in the groups I know, for members to take hands at the end and then quietly to give healing to anyone present who needs it—several together giving the laying-on of hands. This both deepens the atmosphere of love and also gives practice in healing to the group members. It is simply an extension of what has gone before (sending out healing) and conveys the blessing of the living silence of communion with the divine in a special way to someone.

I have only once myself been present when charismatic singing has taken place, as I do not belong to a tradition where this is likely to occur. I found this immensely powerful spiritually, and I wished I might be further involved in it. I do myself just occasionally find the gift of tongues comes to me, but unless I am alone I do not express it. While a Quaker meeting for worship accepts most ministry, this would certainly be unacceptable! Tongues (that strange verbalization of the spirit that travels beyond reason) together with bodily shaking (after which Quakers were originally named), seem rather to belong to *the journey into inwardness* than to the

102

deep and still centre of arrival. For this reason the established spiritual life is perhaps less liable to produce such phenomena than that which is in its earlier stages. But this is to hazard a guess, and certainly I know healers (in particular a close friend who is a Catholic) who always precede the giving of healing with speaking in tongues, if necessary under the breath so that the one receiving cannot hear. This may well help them to centre down quickly and be assured the Spirit is flowing.

Personally I always start with deep breathing, asking the Holy Spirit to breathe within my breath, and after a short while I picture (and usually see) the Light of the divine. This centres on the third eye and travels to the heart, which I picture as a flower of light opening for the light to flow forth from it to those in need. I usually spend almost half the time in the introductory period in entering the Light, and some minutes at the end in consciously closing the heart centre and returning to my ordinary state. However, there are as many ways *in* as there are those who heal and pray.

I have been very fortunate over the years in my prayer companions. During the past few years I have visited a vicar's wife in a neighbouring village, and once a week at nine in the morning we meet for an hour. This weekly occasion has turned into a precious prayer partnership in which we remember the needs of the village, our friends and our families. I am particularly blessed in this friendship because while I am a Light-centred type of soul, my friend is a very Jesus-centred one. Together we enter into one another's experience, and while she sometimes sees Light when with me, several times I have very directly known the presence of Jesus of Galilee. On one of these occasions, Jesus seemed to both of us to be sitting on the third chair in the room, and on another we felt his holy hands laid on our heads in blessing. This for me is a very different experience from that of the Cosmic Christ—much more intimate, personal and human, and teaches me something about the truth known by the evangelicals.

Another group to which I belonged, which ran for about six years, I myself started as an experimental meditation group, and during the last three years this became largely a healing group, drawing to it a number of people with a special healing vocation. Others of us then found our own gifts strengthened there and we knew very close and intimate shared communion of spirit. Such groups as these are very precious, perhaps one's most precious possession of all, and they provide support in a marvellous way in times of suffering and adversity. These webs of relationship are the very stuff of the Kingdom of Heaven and their closeness provides a means of sending out healing far beyond their confines.

Such groups are not easy to establish, but one way to begin is to open oneself inwardly in desire. I certainly did this when originally I founded the experimental meditation group, praying for something of the kind to come about for a year or more before the hope was realized. Then those who formed the group were people just around me whom previously I would not have thought of asking. Where one has a need oneself, often others in fact have it too, and the Spirit may draw us together *when one begins to be aware enough to ask.* Healing arises from sharing. Love and the ministry of healing is based upon that.

Again, convalescence from illness is really assisted by seeking out a place to stay where love and prayer are flowing. In the Friends Fellowship of Healing we have two such guest-houses—Claridge House in Surrey and Lattendales on the edge of the Lake District. Those who run them are not necessarily specially endowed with healing gifts, yet healing and blessing do really flow there, as the many letters of thanks the houses receive demonstrate. Our own homes should be such places too, so that when people visit us they feel an atmosphere that warms and blesses.

I witnessed long-term healing of the psyche taking place at the Quaker Centre for Study and Contemplation at Pendle

104

Hill, near Philadelphia, where I spent a term a few years ago. Here, some forty students came for up to a year at a time, to sort out their lives and re-find their perspectives. All ages of people, from school-leavers to those in their eighties shared life in community, attending only two or three seminars a week while following their own studies and prayer life. The daily meeting for worship, gardening, cooking, housework and washing up were also part of life. Crafts too of many kinds were an important aspect of daily living. Thus the intellectuals often discovered release in meditation, writing poetry, music, contemplation, painting, weaving or pottery, while manual or office workers found intellectual excitement in study. This sort of centre is part of the whole-making that society itself desperately requires, and those who have tasted it are likely to go out as its ambassadors.

It seems that where Quakers put down roots, centres like this tend to arise. I have been fortunate, too, in visiting Viittakivi International Centre in Finland to teach in the summer seminar, and also in going to our English Woodbrooke—both of which, though they have their own special flavour, are doing the same work as is Pendle Hill. Woodbrooke welcomes both Friends and non-Friends, for short courses on the principles and practice of Quakerism, and also on the nurture of the spiritual life. Biblical and Peace Studies are also on offer and opportunity is given for a multitude of interesting investigations into such subjects as psychology, feminism and the frontiers of theology and politics. Its description of itself is an accurate one:

a place to stop;
a place to stop and think;
a place to stop and think and share with others.

## Healing of the Deep Memories
Most of us have areas of life in some degree blocked by our ability to repress into the unconscious what has been painful

to bear, and often this has happened at a very early age indeed, so that we cannot any longer reach the cause of our distress. This discovery has formed the basis of modern psychology. Wholeness has therefore to reach back into the early days of childhood where insecurity and fear caused the opening of life to be blighted.

A great deal of experience has now been gained about the relieving of early traumas, and it is one of the features of the New Age life that the expensive analysis by a psychiatrist, which necessarily has to be kept for the few, is now able to be shared in group work of all sorts.

I myself have experienced a number of different types of these, which bring about the surfacing of the deep memories. These include Gestalt, Ira Progoff Journal Keeping and deep massage. I have in a very limited way too (when I visited Finland regularly and knew my group at a Yoga centre well) helped people to re-enter their childhood experience, allowing what was painful, as well as early joy and spontaneity, to surface. This proved very therapeutic for some.

Breakdown is *refusal* as well as *inability* to contact the blind layer within, and this not only affects the original damping down of an incident long ago, but prevents the flow of life's energies in everyday living now. As Eckhart, the medieval German mystic, wrote, we have layers as hard as bearskins and oxhides which cover the soul and prevent its contact with the divine flow.

The new culture-patterns give hope that it may be possible so to remove some of these inner blockages that we are put in touch with our feelings, and creativity, mysticism, poetry and renewal of life become real. It is no accident that today it has often been the young in whom the powers of the planet are fully alive, who have been the leaders in the practices of inner discipline which help the intuitive self to operate.

In fact, due to the over-emphasis on the rational in all spheres of life, we are largely a blocked culture. Even though

106

we understand very well in our heads that present courses are leading to ruination of much that is precious, fear causes us instinctively to tighten the blocks even more (like rabbits caught in a snare!) until any change at all in basic life-style appears menacing. For this reason anyone who starts to allow the wider self of intuition free play (even though this may feel like going crazy at first) is on the road to helping break down the illogical logic which undergirds our more psychotic strands of culture.

It is this area of hidden trouble which both Agnes Sandford[33] and later Francis McNutt have pioneered from the charismatic healing angle. Both these writers tell of ways of helping those in need to relive childhood memories while in a prayer state, and bring the figures of Mary or Jesus to heal and make whole the deep memory. This may safely be done in small groups where there is a sensitive leader who can pass on the help that he or she has received from the divine. Heavy-handed guidance or guidance that is unaware of the nuances of others' inner journeying may enter dangerous territory and do damage. Mass inner journeyings of the kind I have had described to me by friends who have spent months in the Bhagwan Rajneesh's ashram in India, while they seem certainly to release many and set them on the road to inner growth, also as certainly so injure others that the mental hospital has to be their next port of call.

For my own inner healing the Quaker meeting for worship is above all where I go for renewal. Week by week to enter the silence of inner seeking with a fellowship of those I know and trust allows the soil of the week to be cleansed and my tensions released. As the years pass there come to the surface from time to time deep challenges from within, which in a painful way reorientate my life. This reorientation comes at its own speed and in its own time under the direction of the spirit, and as it comes, my meeting for worship provides a background of safety.

Quaker worship is a corporate act which encourages, by the stillness of inner surrender, the free flow of the energies of body, mind and spirit. It is curious how others may give one help by speaking directly the needed advice, or by setting off a train of thought which leads to the answer. The experience of the silence is strangely personal; communion together may often be very tender, in the sense that one feels one has been approached with great tenderness of spirit. I sometimes think that if more Friends consciously thought of those they knew who need healing and pictured the divine love surrounding and penetrating them, they would use their time together even more fruitfully.

In the surrender to intuition as practised by Friends too, *the will* is rightly engaged. Simply to remove inner blocks so that the wider self of intuition can have free play is not only insufficient, but also may lead to *an undoing* which is not the counterpart to finding new wholeness. Desire for goodness, love and an ability to do the will of the divine and so find fulfilment, is the polarity needed when one ventures into the unknown within.

It is this breaking down isolated from some picture of fulfilment in very many people which causes havoc. Just to let go may be to let go not to the constructive forces which have been seeking release, but to the despairs, frustrations and death-wishes hidden within. These indeed have to be recognized as ours, but only in relation to our place in the redemption of the planet.

**Healing in Society**
The deprived in the world and in our own society are many and include those who have been irreparably damaged by lack of love and security at an early age. As the twilight areas of our cities increase through lack of adequate planning and rebuilding, society falls into real danger. Unemployment and broken families have sown the wind and may cause us to reap the

whirlwind. However, **there really is** such a thing as *amazing grace* that can reach down to heal the warped personality that is only too liable to seek its fulfilment in crime. This amazing grace needs to be linked with imaginative expertise. The key is in believing it possible that there might be betterment. When someone dares to believe in us, often this is the beginning of daring to believe in our own better possibility.

I have been privileged over many years to be on the committee of Glebe House, a small Quaker home for maladjusted boys, who come there for a few months to a year or two on leaving school. As times become harsher, the forms of maladjustment reaching the Community become more severe, and often one feels that so much hurt has been done that the personalities are beyond much basic improvement.

I was touched recently when the wardens, Rodney and Mary Smith (who have held the position for fourteen years), remarked that they believed there was no longer any form of wickedness, sexual deviancy or frozen inner being which could appal or repel them, but that at the same time they now realized that there are no stock answers: only fresh creativity given in love could answer the questions posed by the bizarre suffering of these young people.

Health and escape into sanity have to arise time and again new-minted out of relationship, and as we dare to interrelate at depth we extend further our reach. For many of those severely wounded in babyhood the problem is to manage to relate *at all*, and then it is necessary for someone to take the risk of trying to approach the sufferer in his or her isolation. The healing of the deep hurt that we call maladjustment needs long, slow endurance with patient commitment in the day-to-day life, by those who attempt it.

How much more then is this not true of the healing of the maladjusted societies? Northern Ireland, whose anguish has gone on for centuries; Palestinians deprived of a home, confronted with Jews with soul-marks left on the descendants of those who died at Auschwitz and Buchenwald? Here is all the sickness of the maladjusted child writ large into a social grouping affecting thousands.

It is here that prayer is desperately needed. There is indeed enormous spiritual power which may be channelled directly into our world by those who surrender themselves in holy obedience. I believe the need is to offer oneself to be taught how best to do this, as certainly the gift of so doing has to come in from beyond. Such prayers never go unanswered, and perhaps we begin to pray for them as the call to the vocation is heard.

For me the New Paradigm has brought realization that the small part that each one plays in the redemption of society's smallest and least, oldest and most deprived, is work for the whole, and to value what it is *to be human* is an end in itself.

A holistic approach to health is an approach which provides an atmosphere which is life-enhancing. There is a network of relationship which binds all things together for the planet's unseen purpose—this is a purpose of loving which will draw the human race and its environment into closer unity.

### Unusual Healing Events

Certain happenings in my life connected with healing stand out as indicators of the power of the spirit functioning in unusual ways. These point to possibilities in the New Paradigm which I have simply to record without explanation.

One of these occurred when I was staying at Saarijarvi Yoga Centre in Finland teaching a course on *Healing and Yoga*. That year the course was attended by a small group of healers who came from the remote country in northern Finland. They were simple people—three women and a man. Within a day or two, we all realized that there was a powerful spiritual presence among us which seemed to centre on Davitte, their leader. Davitte (I failed to learn his surname) had been a healer all his life, and as old age approached he suffered a

110

severe stroke. He appealed to the Lord either to heal him so that he could continue to be useful or to take him into the next world. This resulted in a vision of Jesus Christ and his complete healing and proved to be the start of a deeper healing ministry.

Davitte had been a post office engineering worker and chiefly healed people in the villages near where he lived. Now in retirement he formed a healing group of five, who all lived within a short distance of his home. One of these was Maria (a seamstress) who was very delicate and sensitive and found it hard to spend much time with others in an ordinary way. These friends worked together to heal, finding that they were able to share one another's gifts; for instance Davitte and Maria were enabled in spirit to visit patients who lived at a distance, actually seeing them and in spirit laying hands on them for healing. He explained to us (all had to be translated from Finnish) that, in healing, first he felt a tide of compassion rise within him for the person needing help. Next he opened himself to ask the Lord's forgiveness and help for that person, suggesting, 'Either use me, or perhaps use me as a channel for some other healer, or dear Lord, if it is necessary, then come yourself and bring healing'. The group knew themselves especially to be in touch with a Finnish doctor in the next life who used to live in South Finland, whom they had not known during his earthly life, but who gave them help in healing when necessary.

The following year during my stay in Finland, again taking the healing course, I bathed in the lake when the water was very cold—and half an hour later while leading a group meditation, my memory failed! My companions phoned my husband who was in another part of Finland, and he directed them to wait at least until morning (it was then 5.30 p.m.) as this had happened once before when I fell into the Cambridge river in early April. On that occasion my memory restored itself after about three hours.

The next thing that I knew was lying in bed at 1 o'clock in the morning with the thought 'My mind is not functioning, but I am safe in God's hands. Yes! I am in Finland, therefore I should seek the aid of Davitte and Maria . . .'. Then immediately I felt their presence with me and Davitte's hands on my head giving me healing—and then my mind cleared. I told Elvi Saari (my dear Quaker mentor) who was spending the night with me, and she replied that she was not surprised as they had phoned him at 9.30 the previous evening. We slept through until morning and then phoned Davitte again. He said yes, he knew I was healed, and that he had had difficulty in getting through to me with healing, and knew just when it occurred: 'I was there with you both in spirit, and after she was better, I went back to bed'.

This connection with the Finnish healing group is still very important in my life, and while I met them just that one week and it is some years ago, our lives I believe are deeply intertwined. Spiritual vitality flows between us.

Maria has the ability to see the light vibrations and inner spiritual essence in people and she did trance-state readings for some of us. This was a moving experience, and while Maria had no notion about my husband's life or his mind, she spoke of his having extraordinary huge mind-structures which were helping to bring together earth and heaven! As he is a mathematical/physics thinker whose lifework has been attempting to put together a theory which can scientifically interpret such things as telepathy and charismatic healing, this was a heart-warming message to receive.[34]

Another instance many years ago, which illustrates the prayer potential of a Quaker Meeting, involved what I believe to have been an angelic presence. We had staying with us from Germany a friend who had been having an agonizing experience, resulting in her father and her husband actually believing that she was a witch. She told me that she was having her vitality sapped by their fear and hate-thoughts, and wondered

112

if she would have a nervous breakdown. I was at the time engaged in hard times with our Night Shelter and felt I had no ability to give her spiritual help. However, while she was staying, it happened that several people came to the house and, apropos of nothing, started recounting to her the help that had come to them through me! This gave her hope and I said I was sure that it was no accident that she had come to stay with us. Somehow the Lord would come to her aid. She was a Catholic (not very dedicated), but after I had explained what Quaker worship was about, she came along to a meeting. Meanwhile I had phoned my Friends Fellowship of Healing group members asking for their special prayer-help for my friend.

We had not been more than a minute or two in meeting, when I found myself carried deep into the Living Presence (a thing I had been unable to reach for a long time) and the opening seemed to include my friend at my side. About half-way through meeting (which had been silent) a tremendous Light Presence came to me, and I even opened my eyes for a second in case the room had been flooded with spiritual Light. I thought to myself *This is an Angel*, and then the words came to me: 'He that is with you is stronger than those who are against you'. When the meeting ended, I took my friend's hand and asked her if she had profited. Then we discovered we had shared the whole experience. It was important for her that I was able to authenticate her experience, and from this flowed better things. When she returned home to Germany, her husband (from whom she was separated) phoned her to say that it was strange, but he had actually fantasized that she was involved in witchcraft, and all sorts of nonsense—he was not even sure why now! But anyway it was all over, and couldn't they meet to discuss how best to help their children? Those in the meeting who had brought about this happening through their prayers were not even aware of it. This I think is often the case when we pray for others.

I do not know if I have a guardian angel, but I assume so—(again what that means I hardly know). Certainly I have helpers in the other world, now including my own mother, and the sister superior of my convent school. This latter was borne out by the fact that lately, attending a course on Complementary Medicine at my local village college, a member of a spiritualist healing group said to me that she could see two 'sisters of mercy' with whom she believed my spirit was linked. She was not sure whether they were in this world or the next! She then produced their names, one of which is *Benedicte*, which she offered in an embarrassed way as being so strange. Of these two, one is in fact in *this* world, and one in the *next*. Neither had been in my mind for months, and I had not asked for a reading when the lady told me. She got the name of the other sister correct as well.

The healing of our world I am sure lies in our ability to interrelate with one another. *The communion of saints* is something that should be taken for granted, and if we do so, paths open for its further development. Many people know Jesus as their helper in a direct way (I seldom do, though the divine presence I know), so why not also know *the blessed fraternity*? If we are all one in God, surely this is a way in which it would be likely to manifest itself to sensitive awareness?

One of my special vocations has been occasionally giving help to those who have just died and do not find the way to take the next step. Usually these are people who have not acclimatized themselves to any thought of what there might be beyond death and thus seem stuck here unable to depart from their earthly surroundings. At the Night Shelter sometimes I used to know the presence of men who had died, and I always welcomed them by name, silently saying something like: 'Hullo Peter! So you are here. Nice to see you. Other people don't see you, but never mind that! I have a feeling there is something better you could do than be here, and if you look around, there are people who will help you, but you need to reach out to them. Let me help you do that'. After a few days they generally disappeared. You must understand I did not actually *see* them, rather I was aware of their presence, even knowing just where they were sitting.

On another occasion I had a Labour Party councillor friend who was dying, and in my morning quiet time I was made aware of it. I immediately wrote a note to him and his wife which someone put through their door, telling them not to be at all afraid of anything that would happen, because life was much safer than it seemed. I promised I would be with them in spirit all day, while at the same time I was running about electioneering. Actually I was standing as a candidate in a local election that day, and all the time part of me was steadily engaged in holding my friend and his wife safely by the hand in a spiritual way.

He died while I was at the vote-count. The next day I went down to the Scilly Isles for a week's rest, without seeing his wife. However, while I was travelling and for three days after his death, I accompanied my friend in spirit night and day, comforting and supporting him, until he found his way on the other side. On my return, his wife told me that as he had lain semi-conscious that last day while she held his hand, he had kept on repeating *my* name, and when the note came through the door, she understood that I was with them too, holding their hands in mine. This was particularly significant to me because it had been my habit in my quiet time during the preceding weeks, in spirit to take their hands and bring them down into the still place of healing and wholeness.

In the sphere of healing there is very much to learn, and one is grateful for indications that one is rightly guided and able to listen. Last year I was taking a day on Healing and Health at a Friends Meeting in the north of England. This ended with a session where those who felt they would like a special blessing came forward, and several of us together gave them the laying on of hands. Two young mothers sat side by side for this, and I whispered to one to ask if there was any special need. She told me she was an epileptic and also at the present time was suffering the sad loss of a child whom she had cared for since its birth. As soon as I opened myself within, there came a tremendous outpouring of spiritual light and an inner command to *stop immediately*. This I did, gently explaining to the young woman that although the experience had only been one split second, yet she had received a wonderful blessing and should not receive anymore now. This was interestingly borne out by someone else in the room, who did not know the one receiving healing, but felt a panic lest something awful might happen. This was immediately relieved when we removed our hands. I imagine a moment more and she would have started an epileptic fit. Anyway, the blessing was real enough, and she began to come to Friends Meeting, where she found support and help, and the heavy weight of the tragedy which she was carrying was greatly relieved.

My own feeling is that dramatic happenings like the above happen *when the divine can find no other way*. Usually the working of the spirit is hidden, quiet and undramatic.

I personally believe our healing vocation in this world lays the foundation for carrying it on in the next. It is important to train ourselves inwardly here in the channelling of spiritual healing and blessing, so that after we die we shall be able to interrelate in the redemptive process.

# CHAPTER 5

# TIME AND ETERNITY—DEATH AND REBIRTH

## Growing Older

In the East old age is regarded as the time for spiritual growth. Elderly men were encouraged to leave their work and home to pursue the spiritual path. I find this notion attractive. Late middle life may open up possibilities yearned after that there has never been time or space to fulfil, especially if I make sure not to busy-body into activities which at this stage I may leave to others.

It is common, now that health is better and we all tend to live longer, not to regard ourselves as old at sixty or sixty-five. Yet if we are to establish deeper patterns conducive to inner growth, this should be done while we are still in possession of full energy. The younger we start the more we are likely to increase in spiritual awareness.

Many cease to grow spiritually in their twenties, and it is only too easy, as I am finding, to sit back once over sixty and cease to increase in wisdom. Faith is certainly not to be tied up in a tight parcel of 'I believes'. It is a path along which I have to walk into further truth. Inner work depends largely on the realization that there is a potential in humanity that will continue to manifest itself creatively in mysterious and powerful ways, loosing us from the incarceration of self-centredness into fuller participation in life. The way this may happen alters as I grow older.

I find that intimacy with the divine is related to the proportion in which I dare to trust those amongst whom I move daily. I feel a unity with life just in the proportion to which I manage to withdraw into the place of unitive prayer. Spiritual

awareness brings an increasing balance between inner communion and the outer depth of relationship with other people
and the substance of life. A sense of being guided (being 'in
the flow' is the Buddhist phrase for it) allows circumstances, if
I can listen to them, to direct the way I should go. Sometimes
this is patently obvious and sometimes I walk in the dark for
months. The things which are really *for me* come to me.
Something in me draws them, I think, and this causes me to
see myself as part of a life-process (as much as are the stars,
the earth and the animals).

I try to take to myself the Yaqui Sorcerer's advice in *The
Teachings of Don Juan* (Carlos Castaneda's first book):

> The man will be, by then, at the end of his journey in
> learning, and almost without warning he will come upon
> the last of his enemies: Old Age! This enemy is the
> cruellest of all, and the one he won't be able to defeat
> completely, but only fight away.
>
> This is the time when a man has no more fears, no more
> impatient clarity of mind—a time when all his power is in
> check, but also the time when he has an unyielding desire
> to rest. If he gives in totally to his desire to lie down and
> forget, if he soothes himself in tiredness, he will have lost
> the last round, and the enemy will cut him down into a
> feeble old creature. His desire to retreat will overrule all
> his clarity, his power and his knowledge.
>
> But if the man sloughs off his tiredness, and lives his fate
> through, he can then be called a man of knowledge, if
> only for the brief moment when he succeeds in fighting
> off his last, invincible enemy. That moment of clarity,
> power and knowledge, is enough.[35]

The whole point of living is to become spiritually aware in
thinking, feeling, suffering and doing. It is not success so
much that matters any more, as becoming more deeply
human—that is, kinder, truer, more to be relied on and less

automatic in response. It is deadly easy mechanically to tick over without inspiration or creativity. Development and independence come by following desires and natural drives, both in relation to society and in antagonism to it, but the way of all the great religions is in escape from the automatic patterns of 'I want, I need, I have, I will' in order to make room for inspiration, genius and the workings of the spirit of love and truth.

If people are to change gear into a higher use of their mind and body and develop transpersonal (i.e. divine and psychic) awareness, this will lead them not to identify so completely with their outer environment. It is not that the world should be despised or considered unreal, but that one should come to see oneself (and all else too) *as beyond the world* as well as deriving from it. Indeed it is only when this is tasted that the paradisal unity with created things is recovered. This extra sense is the true 'second childhood'—in it too is the discovery that 'there's a divinity that shapes our ends, rough hew them how we will'.

Perhaps C. G. Jung was right when he said half humorously that schools were needed for the middle-aged, because pieces of ourselves remain caught in earlier patterns—and so we fail to take responsibility for life as we should. For instance, psychic fusion with parents can continue all our lives, and rightly to escape from this entails seeing them as real people. To forgive our parents and understand how much they had to bear from us as children, is one of the keys to becoming mature.

I personally am aware of following my own mother's (and grandmother's) pattern in choosing someone to marry whom I both respect and in many ways, in outward things, dominate—my daughter is doing the same. Is this 'imprinting' (as happens with baby birds)—or something in the ultimate essence of us?

I suppose old age is my last chance both to gain that fluid

thing Jung calls 'individuation' and to put right the wrong decisions of my life. Here, it is clear that those who *have*, to them is added, while those who *have not* are only too liable to have taken from them the rest of what they possess. It takes courage for a hyperactive like myself to enter upon a quiet lifestyle unfettered by responsibilities, so that I may conserve spiritual energy and begin to live with contemplative awareness.

I see my approaching old age as the beginnning of a new kind of living. I hope I have managed to draw together the past so that it may to a great extent be released and left behind. This book is part of it. I understand that I am no longer playing the roles I used to: I am *not* the mother of a large family, I am *not* a full-time peace worker, I am *not* a weighty Friend, I am *not* a county councillor, I do *not* work with alcoholic vagrants. I am *not* the first woman secretary of the Council of Churches in my town. If someone asks what I do—these are not the answers I now give. On the other hand, I do want above all to be *used* by the Inner Christ to remake the patterns of this beautiful world, and I believe the best way to pursue the spiritual path is likely still to be based in the heart of everyday living. All this feeling of 'I am not' is not a cop out. It is a desire to find a way to be baptized more and more deeply into living, in ways I have not known before.

My own mother is an example to me. After an outgoing public life carried on while bringing up a large family, she became an oblate of an Anglican order of sisters. Her day at home was latterly structured by the regular offices of an ancient liturgy which provided a rhythm both for day and for those times in the night when (like many old people) she awoke in a desolation of loneliness. This practice of the semi-monastic life in her own home turned her loneliness into right solitude, but my word—*how she did talk* when any of her family turned up to see her! In other words her surface self was sometimes really starved, but at the same time I never felt

120

when I left her that she would feel miserable. I had fed her with talk and she was ready to go back into her monastic silence again.

She was not alone in spirit because she came close to others in prayer—much closer I think than many do in actual face to face meeting. She used to say she thought it was her special vocation to use old age as further training in being a channel and catalyst for spiritual help. Being of a systematic turn of mind, she kept a notebook of those for whom she prayed, with sections for daily, weekly and monthly lists; these included family, friends, organizations with which she had worked, and people she heard of in the newspaper.

Increasingly her power to channel blessing grew. As she put it to me once when she was eighty: 'My inner radio is improving these days'. We kept in close touch when I was working in the Night Shelter, and in times when things became violent, I was very aware of her being 'plugged in' to what was going on there, and phone calls next morning would prove the truth of it. Incidentally, I sensed this even more strongly after she had passed into the next life.

At one time she phoned me to say that she had felt one of our sons, who was staying on a kibbutz in Israel, had been in dire need: 'I dropped everything I was doing and held on for him inwardly for about four hours and then it seemed that all was well. Whether that means he has now passed into the next life or that the crisis is over, I am not very sure'. Soon after this a letter arrived from Israel to say that our son had nearly drowned at that time, having gone bathing in a dangerous place where the rocks were too slippery to gain handhold, and thus he found himself unable to get out again. The boiling sun overhead made him feel faint and at the same time he felt too tired easily to swim or float. He wrote that several times he had nearly let himself drown, until finally someone walked by and managed to help him out. I feel sure that my mother both provided additional

121

spiritual energy for him and was in some way involved in the whole happening.

## Loneliness, Solitude and Inner Power

Loneliness is *a state of mind.* I was amazed how lonely I was during the fortnight that my husband was in hospital. I found I could not be bothered to cook and the evenings proved oppressively long. If I went to bed early I woke up in the night, and I was quite unable to follow my own good advice about seeking the solitude of the saint or the poet. I had my morning's hour of quiet and increased this to a further hour in the evening, but there was such inner distress at being alone I felt no comforting.

At the same time I *do* know that true listening to others arises out of solitude and is a creative act linked to leisure of soul. Certainly a living exchange includes also one's own aches, pains and sorrows, but it needs to lead on to 'Now that's over and let's hear all about *you*'. One feels heartily ashamed on leaving a friend's house in the realization that one has not let them get a word in edgeways. This is so absolutely not what one intended! However, it has to be faced that the lonely *are* garrulous and, like my mother, they may really need to 'outpour'. As I am ready to receive such outpouring and do not consider it a form of greed in relationship when there is real need, then perhaps I need not be too angry with myself when I too succumb to the temptation! However, to deny this need and really to listen is an asceticism on a small scale which can bring the reward of much deeper realization of how others enjoy and suffer. I am sure too that it is only to those who give out a vibration of leisure of soul that confidence is comfortably given, with trust that the whole conversation will not be used as material for the next one.

Power of the inner kind increases with use. It is not unusual for telepathy to develop between those who are close to each other in love. Again, prayer groups increase prayer power, and as the bonds of friendship and trust develop, charismatic healing gifts arise. This type of spiritual study and prayer fellowship has been the most precious part of my life for many years. Such groups sustain and bind people together so that when one falls ill, feels depressed or suffers a bereavement, he or she may count upon the friendship of the others. It is this kind of relationship, where there is both giving and receiving at an inner level, which sometimes extends beyond the grave.

'The Communion of Saints' is a well-known experience to quite ordinary people, and while I believe spiritualistic recalling of the dead may be unwise (in that much in the psychic world to us is murky and uncertain), to rejoice in the awareness of the presence of a loved one is fine. I personally have only very occasionally seen someone who has returned to me, but much oftener I know them as a presence in communion with me, sometimes with a very direct message. Thus I was very glad the other day to read in an article by Martin Israel[36] that when our loved ones,

> come to us in visions or dreams they assume a form we can still recognize. Indeed, this is how they may show themselves to those who are rather obtuse spiritually. Those who are more spiritually aware know their loved ones in pure thought or mental energy. When the so-called 'dead' come to me, as they do quite frequently, they come as a shaft of intelligence. They announce themselves to me in pure thought, and I know them and listen to what they impart. What they tell me is always relevant. And this is the way in which the risen ones always work. They are still part of us, and yet not separate in any way from the true Being of Christ in us. This is what constructive human activity is about. We are aspiring towards a participation in the full power of Christ. Only when our psychic sensitivity is so cleansed

that we can present a perfect instrument whereby the Holy Spirit can come through the Communion of Saints and the ministry of angels to the world of matter, can we ourselves participate in the transformation of the world.

\*     \*     \*

As I look back I see that time and again it has been pain and loss that brought home my inauthentic style of living and pushed me into the perilous and live-giving paths of the spirit. This happens when one has taken the plunge of discipleship and glimpsed the mysterious richness of the divine. When that has happened, then God becomes the centre by which everything is judged. I am going to suffer in any case (as well as create and enjoy) and my freedom lies in choosing to allow my destiny to cause me to evolve. It is the pressure and pain of living, as well as the drawing power of the future which forces me to give up one set of aspirations for a higher. As I dare to follow this way, awareness increases. But to change the way one looks at life at all basically *is* agony, because in doing so one loses one's security, one's place in life, and even one's friends, and has to begin over again. Berdyaev was right when he wrote: 'Safe lives belong to shopkeepers, not to spiritual men'. Most of the time I find myself a shopkeeper!

## The Opening Doors of Old Age

Of course I do not feel old, but I am now over sixty and I begin to see that most old people do not understand that they are old. It delights me to have a friend of 75 who has just returned from a visit to central China on an archaeological trip; another of 80 who recently went out to St Kilda in a smallish boat to watch birds—despite the fact that one can seldom land there because of the wildness of the sea (No! they failed to land). One ought to be like that—undeterred.

124

This means deciding that it really does not matter if one comes back or not. Having reached that conclusion, it should give one the ability to grant space to one's partner to do likewise and in that lies the fine edge between recklessness and being happy-go-lucky.

When I visited Pir Vilayat's Sufi camp in the French Alps the last time, my husband had already started to suffer with high blood-pressure and an enlarged heart. While I did make adequate provision for him, yet had he fallen suddenly ill or died, I would have been difficult to contact quickly. While we were both aware of this, we felt no particular tension. Again, last time we visited Saarijarvi Yoga Centre in Finland, we knew quite well that his body was not up to scratch; the place was remote and the life there rough. As it turned out, the more he carted the branches of trees in the hot sun, the more his health improved! In any case, there, alongside us was the amazing Quaker, Elvi Saari (*Esko* to her friends). Already at 70 and following a serious operation for cancer, she was leading a week on Meditation, Yoga and Forest Clearance! She did not spare herself and neither did the rest of us! The sense of spiritual as well as bodily exhilaration repaid the venture well.

I do believe that old age can cause unknown inner transubstantiation, and the diminishments may be taken as the test of 'God the Amazing Guru'. It is the fiery tests of life that can cause pieces of our inner mechanism to begin functioning for the first time; tests that turn into *Initiations*.

God—seen as the sacred fire of nature, who refuses himself at one level in order to realize himself at another.

God—the tester, who is also God realizing himself in us.

Natural compulsions resisted or denied can either dry up inner being or open up a much richer fountain of life reaching beyond the natural world.

There is a difference between *accepting fate* and *wrestling with it so that it may yield up spiritual fruit*. One does not know if one will be strong enough so to wrestle, but 'God's strength is made perfect in weakness'.

There is no doubt that if I am to change and mature and at the end look back on a fulfilled life, the process of becoming has to continue until the last. Times of tribulation rightly accepted make room for new sprouts of being. Indeed the great Western archetype of *the cross and resurrection* can be the sustaining symbol not only for Christians, but also for those who say no creed.

Both to struggle with hard circumstance and to accept what may not be remedied may well together bring discovery that in mysterious ways it is true that 'all things work together for good to those that love God'. This *'good'* is *inner growth*. This kind of passive acceptance is certainly no negative thing, rather it opens inward doors to those 'strange flowers of myself' that D. H. Lawrence wrote of in his poem 'Shadows',[37] written about old age and its diminishments.

> And if, in the changing phases of man's life
> I fall in sickness and in misery
> My wrists seem broken and my heart seems dead
> and strength is gone, and my life
> is only the leaving of a life:
>
> and still, among it all, snatches of lovely
> oblivion, and snatches of renewal,
> add, wintry flowers upon the withered stem,
> yet new strange flowers
> such as my life has not brought forth
> before, new blossoms of me:
>
> then I must know that still
> I am in the hands of the unknown God,
> he is breaking me down to his own oblivion
> to send me forth on a new morning, a new man.

The surrender of all that we are, to be purified by the spark of the divine, is something we cannot achieve just by willing it, though unless we do go on desiring it, it certainly cannot happen. Purification was what Blake was talking about when he spoke of the cleansing of the doors of perception: 'If the doors of perception were cleansed everything would appear to man as it is, infinite. For man has closed himself up, till he sees all things thro' narrow chinks in his cavern'. And this was Blake's opposite:

> To see the World in a Grain of Sand
>   And a Heaven in a Wild Flower
> Hold Infinity in the palm of your hand
>   And Eternity in an hour.

After any prolonged silence (even a day or two, and much more so, after a fortnight) I find that the *suchness* in creation reveals itself memorably. Just lately, at a short retreat at Bradford-on-Avon, I came out of five hours in the darkness of a 15th-century chapel to find a marvellous enrichment in my seeing. The food we shared was holy, the music was angel's singing, and my eye was caught and held by two tall apple trees whose topmost apples had eluded plucking; the near tree's fruit was brilliant red and the further one, a brilliant green; they dangled deliciously against dark branches swaying in the boisterous wind. I felt this whole scene to be expressive of something in the divine mind which could not *be* in any other way, and the knowledge came with exhilaration.

It struck me forcibly then that actually we cannot help anyone else at any time unless we are in life's pattern to do so. Therefore we have to interfere as little as possible, and only then when it comes from an inward listening. This provides one's real freedom and unity with nature, and it is different from feeling part of a great machine. The inward listening makes one *accountable*, but not a *busy body*.

Purification has to do with being in the divine process

consciously. If I am very aware *that I do not love much*, the way is *not* to try to love more, so much as to spend more time in trying to open myself *to receive the love of God*. The rest takes care of itself.

One way of coming to terms with events that shaped us so that we can fully live in the present, is in consciously and systematically giving way to the desire to relive the past. Many of these old tapes of memory are pleasant and a joy to experience, but as I know to my cost from the experience I had commonly with groups in Finland, for some people to relive early childhood may be very painful. It is in fact surprising how many of us shut off that time as being too hard to bear, even if we did not (as many Finns did) grow up in a country that was being invaded, with food scarce and danger plentiful. All kinds of tensions and anxieties in later life arise from hidden and buried childhood sorrow.

It is one of the Buddhist forms of meditation consciously to relive periods of one's life in this way, allowing memories to surface which carry with them not only joy and satisfaction, but also suffering and feelings of guilt. In doing this, the point is to allow the emotions of long ago to be felt all over again, and at the same time to understand that the true self is separate from what happened. One feels responsible, but from it comes 'recollection in tranquillity'.

The teaching of psychiatry is related to dealing with the present by increasingly understanding and taking responsibility for the past. Christian tradition too with its emphasis on penitence and forgiveness aims at leaving behind bitterness, guilt, and the rest, so that a new lease of life and energy may flow. Looking back can also cause one to see that sometimes one felt appalling guilt and fear over such very stupid things. I have met men who have committed terrible crimes, and when I heard their life story (told me sometimes in the middle of the night by the light of a candle!) I could not feel any surprise. The guilt was a shared one. The crimes arose

128

out of a chain of sad and angry circumstances, and only a better chain in which there is love, forgiveness and hope can raise man's state. Life is evolving in us and has not advanced far in some places.

As a result of meditation I have known deep eruptions of consciousness, with everything in my early childhood welling up from the depths to be relived with great poignancy—especially my love/hate relationship with my mother. I understand now just how right were Jung and the Chinese tradition in seeing that within us (as within the world too) everything has its opposite, its shadow side. Once one has really grasped that, or been grasped by it, life becomes much easier to accept. As Shakespeare's plays illustrate—madness and genius, hell and heaven, life and death, are never far from any of us, even the sanest (perhaps most of all the sanest).

## Facing the Approach of Weakness and Death

We live on the edge of eternity and know it either as mystery or as the void. As the void, it is death. As mystery, it points beyond death. There is indeed a death we have to die, but as is said by the Sufis, it is possible *to die before death*. In fact life invites us to do just that. If we do not succeed in it, the void awaits us and cannot be by-passed. Once that is grasped, one is liable (if one has a violent temperament) to rush into that void recklessly with closed eyes. (Is that to commit suicide? Or to make some heroic act of self-crucifixion? Or? Or?) Later on one comes to see that there is no need for those kinds of dramatics: they hinder. All that is needed is to allow *Life to Live You* instead of perpetually imposing on life. How is that done? I suppose there is an end at some point of believing that to impose oneself works, and in the void that then confronts one—the jump happens. I only know this by inference. I have experienced it

129

partially, but even that partialness took all that at the time was mine.

Jacob Boehme long ago wrote: 'Heaven is nothing else but willing and working in quiet love'. How serene that sounds. Yet it includes the working through of every crisis and the revealing of every hidden secret, as well as the acceptance of what Teilhard de Chardin called our 'passivities'—old age, illness and death. But Teilhard taught *Resist!* Resist everything that diminishes yourself and the world, and then when the point comes where resistance does not help—*Accept* and allow life to have its way with you, knowing that the divine life is the resurrected life.

> To adore . . . that means to lose oneself in the unfathomable, to plunge into the inexhaustible, to find peace in the incorruptible, to be absorbed in defined immensity, to offer oneself to the fire and the transparency, to annihilate oneself, and to give of one's deepest to that whose depth has no end.[38]

and this:

> When the signs of age begin to take my body (and still more when they touch my mind); when the illness that is to diminish me or carry me off strikes from without or is born within me; when the painful moment comes in which I suddenly awaken to the fact that I am ill or growing old; and above all at that last moment when I feel I am losing hold of myself and am absolutely passive within the hands of the great unknown forces that have formed me; in all those dark moments, O God, grant that I may understand that it is You (provided only my faith is strong enough) who are painfully parting the fibres of my being in order to penetrate to the very marrow of my substance and bear me away within Yourself.[39]

> You are the irresistible and vivifying force, O Lord, and because Yours is the energy, because of the two of

us, You are infinitely the stronger, it is on You that falls the part of consuming me in the union that should weld us together. Vouchsafe, therefore, something more precious still than the grace for which the faithful pray. It is not enough that I should die while communicating. Teach me to treat my death as an act of communion.[40]

There are simple ways in which it is possible to prepare the body and mind for the spirit's release into the larger world beyond death. Learning to say goodbye to outworn roles starts back in middle age. As parents we have to see our children grow up and depart into the world. Retirement takes away a life-time's occupations, and the body gradually becomes unable to be so active. It comes with a sense of surprise at first to discover I cannot do everything I thought of (or at least, not without paying for it next day!). I do not want always to wait to be pushed off dead positions; I would rather be one step ahead, listening to life's message that I must find new paths.

The practice of inner silence and the constant attempt to enter into communion with the present moment teach the skills needed to float on the waters of existence when the perils of increasing weakness and age approach. In prayer one is borne up and connected with an invisible environment out of which resources from the unseen world flow in creatively. Each deprivation then may be found to be the necessary stripping undertaken by the mountain-climber, who, at every hut on his journey into the higher altitudes, finds a depot for what must be left behind.

Another preparation for inner growth is to seek a fresh unity with nature. *Being where you are* is a contemplative state which is the heart of the mystical life. I should try more often to accept my surroundings as something never before experienced in that way, so that the new and mysterious may reach me from the aliveness of my environment. Being a

131

bird-watcher is a help because I am always subconsciously registering bird-song and bird-calls. Since I took up painting a few years ago, I have been amazed at the subtlety of colour and shape everywhere—ice-patterns on puddles and leaves, tree-shapes and the rhythm of movement in things. But I do not *dwell* on all this sufficiently: to dwell on it, requires *attention*, and attention is a disciplined activity—as much as is dancing. To enter the dance of life more fully requires self-training. It is by no means time-wasting to be quietly aware, for in that awareness one becomes consciously part of the self-consciousness of God.

My husband really ought not to go out in very cold weather because of his heart condition, but what of the restrictions suffered by those who are tied to chair or bed or hospital? Is the idea then to make an effort to live in *participation* in the details of all that happens? Or perhaps it is not so much an effort that is needed, as a *surrender* of an active kind. This is the opposite of the hideous withdrawal so often seen among people in old folk's homes—when the group sits round the walls in passive non-being, refusing any longer to participate. Such surrender into more sensitive awareness may be agonizing because the paltry and disgusting can take on looming proportions, but might it not be possible to see such awareness as part of the world's divinizing process? A bringing of the light down into the depths of life? Might not sparks of love and hope spring up and reveal themselves surprisingly often? Once or twice I have heard hints of this from the very old and bedridden. I remember too the extraordinary rejoicing of the whole ward last week in our mental hospital's Activities Centre, when Joan (whom I had been helping) actually finished and put on a summer dress. This was probably her first creative enterprise for years?

If I have to grow very old and my mind dims, I take refuge in a story in one of Joyce Carey's novels (I cannot trace which one) of an old man whom his family regard as ailing in mind, who, standing at the window looking out, takes no notice that they are calling him to his dinner. The reason he fails to come is because he is deep in contemplation of a tree losing its golden leaves in the breeze; he finds himself identified with it in a curious unity of consciousness, and through this he enters into communion with all life.

A direct approach to the inner life may be had by daily pondering on all sorts of spiritual literature. I find it good to have morning and nightfall 'holy books' out of which I read small passages as I end my quiet time. It matters very much indeed to seek sleep on the right note of being. Certain novels (particularly children's stories) I find provide just the food before sleep. I have a select few which bring serenity and blessing as soon as I open the page. It is wonderful to stay with a friend and to find beside the bed a choice of books of this type—and I take it as a gift of being from hostess to visitor!

I have quite a number of friends who write poetry now in old age, and it takes them to a level below the threshold of words. Some of this poetry I find marvellous! I am only too aware that I could receive much more from music, for in music I sometimes glimpse through cracks into an unknown world within.

Our city (Cambridge) now rejoices in a University of the Third Age focused on the retired and elderly and some 500 of us attend (and give) lectures and seminars on all kinds of subjects. Through my own (Adventures in Inner Space) a small group has found deep friendship with one another which may well prove lasting. To have the mind stimulated in a solid intellectual sense is better than sitting at home doing crosswords!

\*        \*        \*

Meditation and Prayer are the arts of the deep mind and the best things arise out of them. It is interesting that it is increasingly the psychologists who have been teaching people to experience *altered states of consciousness*,[41] although down through the ages this has always been religion's part. The Catholic Mass and Quaker meeting for worship can lead into these states, when the surface mind relaxes and there is an entering into inner awareness of a deeper kind. Eastern disciplines have been catching on here, just because in the West we have lost touch with our deeper selves.

Conscious willing to be still in body and mind may act as a switch to turn on a more passive and peaceful willing, belonging to inner awareness. This may take over automatically to keep out wandering thoughts and distractions, inducing 'the peace that passes all understanding'. Some people find it hard to train themselves to let go in this way. This may be especially true for the intellectual and well-controlled personalities who will not find it easy to relax the discipline and orderliness which have been their fulfilment, in order to learn to trust the inner voice of their wider spiritual selves.

For them (as I know by the anger I sometimes encounter when I lead process meditations) the state can even feel like sinking into disintegration or senility, and the free-running imagery and silence of the void may be felt as a powerful threat to reason. In fact this threat is real insofar as the condition brings with it an undermining of the sovereignty of the surface self, because anyone who identifies exclusively with his mind cuts himself off from his subconscious. Fear has to be endured if the alienation is to be overcome, and the hallmark of success is certainty that one has come home.

To enter the deeper state is to learn how to face any possible deterioration of mind or body coming at a later stage. This is borne out by an experiment done a few years ago in a San Francisco Hospital, using five groups of people to test for fear of death and of losing control of faculties.[42] The tests included death fantasies and words connected with death. The experiment found that two groups (including graduate students in Religion and Psychology) had never experienced altered states of consciousness, while the other three (psychedelic drug users, Zen meditators and American-born Tibetan Buddhists—all of more than three years standing) had done so. What emerged from the experiment was that only those who had had experience of deeper inner states had no fear of the dissolution of their ego, as these had glimpsed life's wider context. It seems that this is what constitutes for most of us the core of fear itself.

It is probably true that *any* average group of graduates training in Religion and Psychology would give a like result, as the emphasis in such training in the West is on knowledge *about* deeper states and seldom on the *release* of them. I believe that until talk stops and awareness well based in the body and mind begins, there cannot be a basic renewal of Western culture-patterns. It is only this which will assist in overcoming the alienation of heart from head, reason from instinct and soul from mind and body. Once ways are found to tap the deep resources within there will be practical results in the healing of the world.

**Different Traditions on the Fulfilment of the Spiritual Life**
As I look ahead to old age and its challenges, I am helped by the consideration of the different traditions on the fulfilment of the spiritual life.

A. H. Maslow the behavioural psychologist, famous for his work on what he called the Peak Experience, in old age in a recorded dialogue with some friends, told how he came to what he called the *Plateau Experience* and how this came to replace his *Peak Experiences*.

> It is to live at a constantly high level in the sense of illumination or awakening or in Zen, in the easy or miraculous, in the nothing special. It is to take rather

135

casually the poignancy and the preciousness and the beauty of things, but not to make a big deal out of it because it's happening every hour.[43]

I suspect that this is a commoner experience than one might suppose. I *aspire* to it and experience it too, but often I fall right down to the bottom of the ladder. Steady illumination does shine out from many old people, and its radiance is evident. Years ago, collecting from door to door for Christian Aid, my little daughter remarked that she thought the young people were nicer than the old: 'But some of the very old ones are really nasty and a few are *the very nicest of all*'. These 'nicest of all' give out a vibration of having come through much and found serenity. This is different from Maslow's experience, but goes alongside it.

I am only too aware that I may feel peace and a sense of the spiritual when all is going well, before having worked through to sufficient self-surrender for this state to be stable. Anthony Bloom (of the Russian Orthodox tradition) gives a moving example of this in his book *The School of Prayer*.[44]

A young woman fell ill with an incurable disease and she wrote me a letter . . . 'since my body has begun to grow weak and to die out, my spirit has become livelier than ever and I perceive the divine presence so easily and so joyfully'. I wrote to her again: 'Don't expect it will last. When you have lost a little bit more of your strength, you will no longer be able to turn and cast yourself Godwards and then you will feel that you have no access to God'. And after a while she wrote again and said, 'Yes, I have become so weak now that I can't make the effort of moving Godwards or even longing actively and God has "gone".' But I said 'Now do something else. Try to learn humility in the real, deep sense of the word . . .'

Humility is the situation of the earth. The earth is always there, always taken for granted, never remembered, always trodden on by everyone, somewhere we cast and pour out all the refuse, all we don't need. It's there silent and accepting everything and in a miraculous way making of all the refuse new richness in spite of corruption, transforming corruption itself into a power of life and a new possibility of creativeness, open to the sunshine, . . . open to the rain, ready to receive any seed we sow and capable of bringing thirtyfold, sixtyfold, a hundredfold out of every seed. I said to this woman 'Learn to be like this before God; abandoned, surrendered, ready to receive anything from people and anything from God'. Indeed, she got a great deal from people, within six months her husband got tired of having a dying wife and abandoned her, so refuse was poured on generously, but God also shone His light and gave His rain, because after a little while she wrote to me and said 'I am completely finished. I can't move Godwards, but it is God who steps down to me'."

*    *    *

In the East, the wisdom of old age is particularly prized and the ancient Chinese religious classic, the *Tao Te Ching*,[45] gives a picture of fulfilment which is measured and mysterious.

> The ancient masters were subtle, mysterious, profound, responsive.
> The depth of their knowledge is unfathomable.
> Because it is unfathomable
> All we can do is describe their appearance.
> Watchful, like men crossing a winter stream.
> Alert, like men aware of danger.
> Courteous, like visiting guests.
> Yielding, like ice about to melt.
> Simple, like uncarved blocks of wood.
> Hollow, like caves.
> Opaque, like muddy pools.

Who can wait quiet while the mud settles?
Who can remain still until the moment of action?
Observers of the Tao do not seek fulfilment.
Not seeking fulfilment.
Not seeking fulfilment, they are not swayed by desire for change.

I talked about T'ai Chi Ch'uan in an earlier chapter, but there is more to say. In the way that Chinese classic, the Tao Te Ching, has a timeless quality, so also has T'ai Chi, the tradition of which was preserved in the Chinese monasteries and among old men, who did it in order to bring the spirit down into the cells of the body. A good picture of its style is given in Al Chung-lian Huang's book *Embrace Tiger and Return to Mountain*.[46]

Al told us to walk 'as if you don't know what's there—maybe it's grass, maybe it's water'. When I did this, tentativeness came into my body and released my mind from its clutching certainty. We held imaginary soap bubbles in our hands and walked with them. Hold them too tight, they break. Hold them too loose, they slip away.

T'ai Chi is a process of learning to flow with the rhythm of life, it is an unlearning of tightness, both terrifying and exhilarating; it is like a change from being battered by the incoming tide to riding in on a surfboard. It is like taking off your clothes and standing in the summer rain. To begin with there is a struggle to commit the movements to memory and with that one-centred concentration demanded by the slowness of the steps, something enters the body and mind from the heart of the flow of the natural process.

\*     \*     \*

Another example from Eastern tradition comes from *The Upanishads*[47] and this again lights up man's intrinsic unity with all nature.

The Tree of Eternity has its roots in heaven above
and its branches reach down to earth.

It is Brahman, pure Spirit, who in truth is called the
Immortal.

All the worlds rest on That Spirit and beyond him no
one can go:

This in truth is That.

The whole universe comes from him and his life burns
through the universe.

In his power is the majesty of thunder. Those who know
him have found immortality.

From fear of him fire burns, and from fear of him the
sun shines.

From fear of him the clouds and the winds, and death
itself, move on their way.

If one sees him in this life before the body passes away,
one is free from bondage; but if not, one is born and dies
again in new worlds and new creation.

As China produced T'ai Chi, as a means of spiritualizing
the body, so India, which gave the Upanishads and the
Bhagavad Gita, in very early times introduced all the forms
of Yoga for the same purpose. Yoga means Union. Much
Yoga is very suitable to learn and practise in old age, especially uses of breathing and forms of remedial movement. The
essence of Yoga is its meditational quality, and for those who
find any practice of quiet hard, to associate it with Yoga
might well be the answer.

When Eastern mystics teach 'Die before death', it is in fact
the death of the ego for which they call. This may happen
gradually and piecemeal over a lifetime of self-giving (I see it
as a lifetime of attempting to be *more human* and to *follow
truth and love* in action and thought), or it may happen in a

series of breakthroughs in consciousness related to and arising from everyday life. Such breakthroughs do not of course signify that the ego is finally dead—indeed we need our egos in some sense in order to live in the world—but they do help a person to understand what ego-death entails, namely, the surrender to life's deepest purposes.

*　　*　　*

A classic Christian example of the death of the ego is that of the 17th-century American Quaker, John Woolman, who in grave illness found himself so near death that he forgot his name.

Desiring to know who he was he saw a mass of human beings in as great misery as they could be and live, and he understood that he was mixed up with them and henceforth might not consider himself as a distinct or separate being. After some hours of this he heard angelic voices talking together and one said *'John Woolman is dead'*. As he returned to consciousness he found himself saying, 'I am crucified with Christ, nevertheless I live, yet not I, but Christ lives in me . . .' and then he perceived the mystery that there is joy in heaven over a sinner who repented, and the words 'John Woolman is dead' meant no more than the death of the will.[48]

For me this passage about Woolman demonstrates clearly that spirituality is much more than any altered state of consciousness, though it may and often does include this further sensitivity. Rather, spirituality is a whole way of life which seeks identification with the divine will. In the Christian tradition the *It* is known as *He* in a living encounter. Sometimes the experience indeed seems to be *Light, Power, Freedom, Unity with the All*, but at others there is a very acute awesomeness of encounter with what is both the heart of what I am, and also utterly beyond that—so that I see myself as a drop in a great sea. So much so that my inner being knows

140

itself in jeopardy of disintegration, and if I do not rush back to the surface in escape, but dare to accept the inflooding of Love, then . . .

Rainer Maria Rilke expressed the terror as well as the joy of such an encounter in the first of his *Duino Elegies*:

> Who, if I cried would hear me among the angelic Order?
> And even if one of them suddenly pressed me against his heart, I should fade in the strength of his stronger existence.
> For Beauty's nothing but the beginning of Terror we're still just able to bear,
> And why we adore it so is because it serenely disdains to destroy us.
> Each single angel is terrible
> And so I repress myself, and swallow the call-note in depth dark sobbing.[49]

All the same I know quite well that I have known times in the past and will again know times in the future when I may not 'repress myself and swallow the call-note'. The call-note will be answered by the whole of what I am, and it is for this that I live and for this that I shall die.

Or again, as I remember how I feverishly searched for spiritual news in my youth, I discovered Thomas à Kempis's warning in *The Imitation of Christ*, 'He who is a searcher after my majesty shall be overwhelmed by the glory of it'.

This is God, seen as the *Tremendum* with whom an encounter causes an awe which amounts to terror, so enormous are His spiritual energies and His purity. In earlier years there were times when my spiritual insulation was ripped off (or worn through) by an overdose of suffering, exhaustion or prolonged time of inner search, and then I was not properly protected from these energies. T. S. Eliot wrote in *The Four Quartets* that man cannot bear very much reality. Once this has been understood the path into an increase of life becomes plainer. For me it has been a great step forward

141

no longer to desire the glorious, the power of the holy, the beauty of majesty, no longer to hope for a spiritual master, or to find a holy place or a sacrament—because increasingly I come to see that the Source of all Life is gradually and unfailingly, quietly and in His own way, making Himself known to me.

Now therefore the advice I give to myself is this:

> I do not know when or how it will please God to give you the quiet mind you need; but I tell you I believe it is to be had; and in the meantime you must go on doing your work, trusting in God even for this. Tell Him to look at your sorrow; ask Him to come and set it right making the joy go up in your heart by His presence.[50]

This is by no means to say that I feel I may not rejoice in the hidden mystery of the divine Beloved and Most Glorious, but rather that in one sense:

> The primary aim of the religious life should be the search for justice, rather than the cultivation of ecstasy, from which it follows that God is to be encountered most fully not in a hidden spiritual world beyond the senses but in history, the moral and political struggle of past and present.[51]

In another sense the opposite polarity has to be held, and it is certainly *not* as Punshon says 'that the primary aim of the religious life, should be the search for justice' because *the primary aim is love.* There is indeed no either/or in the matter between the search for justice and the cultivation of ecstasy—because ecstasy is something that appears within, like falling in love.

I believe that in order to cooperate with the divine in the evolution of the world and its 'divinization', there must be both encounter and loving commitment, but that encounter has indeed to be in history and in the world of action as well as in adoration within the silence of the heart.

# CHAPTER 6

# FINDING A FAITH FOR THE NEW PARADIGM

## Making Bridges between Eastern and Western Spirituality

Certain of us have to be bridge people between the old forms of spirituality and the new, consciously offering ourselves to life for its inner experiments. To be a Quaker provides a particularly solid and open background for this vocation.

It is no accident that at this time there is a spiritual exchange at depth taking place between East and West. Friends have had a tradition over many years of spiritual exchange with those of other faiths, and of recent years this 'mutual irradiation'[52] has been proceeding apace.

My own first taste of Eastern traditions, apart from reading, came from taking up Transcendental Meditation about 1964. TM entails the repetition of a mantra in order to still one's thoughts, so that the deeper mind may be given the chance to take over. I was given the most common Indian one, the repetition of the Sanskrit name of God, Ram, Ram, Ram. I did this half an hour twice a day for six years, occasionally during the first couple of years visiting a 'checker' to ensure that I was not departing from what I had received. This practice taught me in a systematic way how to still the mind: when thoughts came to the surface (as they still continue to do even now), I learned to regard them a moment and try to let them go, refusing to follow in pursuit. I found this purified my consciousness sufficiently to increase the possibility of entering my surroundings in a way that made nature reveal herself more freshly. I was at that time leading a public life as well as running a large household, and the practice made me far more *situation-centred*. Normally I had lived much on the periphery of myself and now I had a better contact with 'the still point of the turning world'.

As time went on I began to glimpse also what is meant by waiting in 'choiceless awareness' (Krishnamurti's phrase). This can either be the attitude of a young child—or of a spiritually mature person. Sometimes we all slip into the child's open awareness and now and again enter the more conscious spontaneity of the saint. This is to be recognized because *conscious spontaneity* breaks down the ordinary stereotypes which prevent us from meeting reality as living and real—we no longer take the ordinary for granted. It makes life much more interesting, more beautiful but also more painful.

However, as happens with many people on the spiritual path at some time, this steady going-forward into increased awareness (which was rooted in both TM and also in Friends meeting for worship) issued in a spiritual blow-out. This came about at a time when I was undergoing severe strain in every-day things: peace work was turning into direct action and I went to prison, our children were in mid-process of agonized growing up, and I was over-involved in County Council work. When I would least have desired it, I was persuaded into taking a hallucinogenic drug (psilocybin)—this was a carefully measured dose by a pharmacological researcher—in fact my own son.

During the experience (about a six-hour one) I kept my spirit steady by the use of the mantra crystal 'Thine' (one I often use while walking about). After some hours of an agon-izingly acute consciousness, in the latter part I saw everyday things lighted up with heavenly beauty from within. Finally, I reached a point where I knew that by this repetition I was not so much abandoning myself to God, as holding fast to a support for my own ego-security. It then appeared to me that I was invited to let go in a moment of judgement. All I had loved and chosen since I was born, as well as all that had been

144

done to me, concluded here, and I thought that if I let go I should die. It was a hard moment of choice and I felt it would be possible to refuse, but in that case I would approach no nearer to my heart's desire. However, if I did relinquish what I was, I guessed that my consciousness would be wiped out. Every security within had to be surrendered and I remember being aware that I was saying a very final goodbye. Thus, squeezing together the remnants of my shattered courage, I managed to abandon myself—and in that instant there came an inrush of spiritual power like a hurricane, followed by a swift change in consciousness, and I found myself in the Light which is our Source and Ground.

This I knew as Love, far and away more loving than its human counterpart, more personal than anything I knew as personality, and yet much more essentially what we are than we are able yet to be. It was not possible for me to remain in that state for more than seconds because all the layers of selfishness which made up most of what I was (anything in fact that was not the eternal spark which momentarily had reunited with its Source) would have disintegrated. So I fell away from the Light into the *me* I usually think of as myself. But as this happened, a voice within me spoke a word of power—'Serve'—and I knew this as the meaning of my existence.

It took me a very long time to work through all that I received in that flash. I understood for myself that everything streams out from a divine centre, so that all we know is instilled with this Divine Light Energy. For months I could not hear the name of God without tears and was abnormally vulnerable to beauty and pain. Everywhere I was confronted with Live Presence, and in between ordinary work I perpetually scribbled in my diary, notes about the secret and mysterious life I saw. In fact I skirted a nervous breakdown, and it was fortunate that the structures of daily living kept on demanding my attention—in other words, *Serving kept me* *sane*! I had not been ripe for what had happened and learnt with bitterness the foolhardiness of trying to burgle what one should patiently wait to receive.*

This acuteness of vision did not last for more than a few months, and all this is now twenty years ago. However, it did provide a new certainty of spiritual truth. I now realized that the symbols, myths and religious doctrines are a poetry describing something utterly real. I was also much more able to differentiate between the extent to which spirituality is *a way of life* and to which it is *a state of consciousness*. I grasped the fact that states of higher consciousness, unless they are well-rooted in human life and in nature, do not heal and mature the personality, much less produce spiritual rebirth. My own mind suffered a severe degree of disorganization and it was only with great difficulty that I managed to hide the fact and go on living normally. Certainly the steadiness of my contact with Friends was a stabilizing factor.

This spiritual knowledge, however, slowly became *something I remembered*, rather than an immediate and living contact, and it was not until twelve years later at a Sufi retreat that I had a natural spiritual experience of the inner Light which left the door of the inner world permanently ajar.

---

* R. E. L. Masters and Jean Houston comment in their book *The Varieties of Psychedelic Experience*,[53] which is a guide to the effects of LSD on human personality that 'Out of our total of 206 subjects we believe that six have had this (introvertive mystical) experience. It is of interest to observe that those few subjects who attain to this level of mystical apprehension have in the course of their lives either actively sought the mystical experience in meditation and other spiritual disciplines or have for many years demonstrated a considerable interest in integral levels of consciousness. It also should be noted that all of these subjects were over 40 years of age, were of superior intelligence, and were well-adjusted and creative personalities. It would appear, therefore, that where there is an intellectual and other predisposition, a belief in the validity of religious and mystical experience, and the necessary maturity and capacity to undergo such experience, then we have the conditions favourable to the psychedelic-mystical state'.

This took place during a fortnight's retreat in which a point came where I was overwhelmed with spiritual fire, which filled first my head and then my heart. In fact my physical heart was very disturbed by it giving me severe palpitations so that I wondered if I was having a heart attack. It was as though I was on fire inwardly and for the next few days I felt I was being shown the meaning of *the Power of Christ*. This appeared to me as *the Incarnated Light* streaming from *the incredible Light and Energy Centre* (which is the Love of God) that pours into every creature and into creation as its real life, and which Jesus so tenderly and with such humility revealed to humanity. This sending-forth is the Word spoken into all Creation, the Cosmic Christ.

This is where both the Gospel of John and the writings of Paul are for me of such inestimable value, giving, as they do, the key to how the redemptive process is becoming conscious in and through people. As with the drug-experience long before, this took me about a year to come to terms with, and it was this time no coincidence that having been travelling widely among Friends for nearly three years (following the giving of the Swarthmore Lecture) I now had a natural rest-period. Even so, sometimes in those ensuing months, I was afraid to enter too deeply into the silence, in case I experienced more than I could endure in the context of home-keeping. However, on this occasion I never felt threatened with nervous breakdown as I had earlier following the drug-taking episode. A further twelve years of meditation and life had prepared my psyche so that this gift gradually settled down into an ability to sense the Inner Light in a simple and ordinary way without strain.

I received this further opening through the blessing of Pir Vilayat Inayat Khan who led the Sufi Retreat Camp. An inspired master can lead those who will dare to follow him to places in the inner realm which they could not reach on their own at that stage—but more of that later on in this chapter.

I share this story in order to make plain that today such things *are happening*, and I personally know a number of ordinary people like myself, who have been experiencing in like manner. We are *not* special people, *not* particularly holy or good; some whom I know are *not* naturally spiritually psychic. It is as though the power of the spirit is becoming more available because the earth has need for it, and it is vital that we do not prevent its work by being certain that it could not happen to us.

The Spirit uses those who respond, not necessarily those most suitable. It is, I sometimes think, more available to the *'small shepherd'* psyches than the *'high magi'* ones, because the latter have been required to think their way through as never before. I actually know one or two people, who are so afraid of spiritual experience at depth that, in resisting it, they actually from time to time fall ill. At times when they pluck up courage to allow it to flow its natural course, they heal others in a dramatic way and themselves find healing. Their fear is rooted in the fact that they are asked to surrender their ego in order to experience the power within. To do this, even momentarily, is hard.

It is interesting that the shamanic traditions of the world provide examples of people finding their vocation through epilepsy, an illness or great dreams. Only if they give themselves over to a guiding from within, is this brought into obedience.

\*　　　\*　　　\*

Death brings us into the Light of the Divine, as I said in my last chapter. When the Sufis teach 'Die before death', it is the death of the ego at which they point. This happens in dramatic ways for dramatic temperaments and more quietly and gradually in gentle ones. Certainly in the opening of a *chakra\** there

---

\* *Chakra.* In Indian philosophy there are psychic spiritual centres situated in the body.

148

seems to be a sense of sacrificing all one possesses for something greater.

For me Teilhard de Chardin sums up one aspect of the Christian vocation:

> On the one hand I want to plunge into the midst of created things and mingling with them, seize hold upon and disengage from them all that they contain of life eternal, down to the very last fragment, so that nothing be lost: and on the other I want, by practising the counsels of perfection, to salvage through self-denial, all the heavenly fire imprisoned within the threefold concupiscence of the flesh, of avarice, of pride: in other words to hallow, through chastity, poverty and obedience, the power enclosed in love, in gold and in independence.[54]

This is comparable to an athlete's discipline as Paul suggested in his letters. If the ballet-dancer has to sacrifice her ordinary life-style in order to train herself—so certainly has the mystic. Perhaps the mystical and inward exploration is *the* most important vital search that the divine is undertaking in our evolution at the present time. We need to confirm one another's experience for this reason. However, to be profitable and secure, without inflation on the one hand and refusal to accept what comes on the other, these explorations have to be based on the search for unity with the Divine Beloved or Ultimate Truth, and never upon curiosity and spiritual power-seeking. There can be a narrow knife-edge here, as the wise Tibetan, Chögyam Trungpa, indicates:[55]

> In order to have the experience now, one would have to give up the evaluation of how wonderful the flash was, because it is this memory which keeps it distant . . . If one searches for any kind of bliss or joy, the realization of one's imagination and dream, then equally one is going to suffer failure and depression . . . So the real experience

beyond the dream world is the beauty and colour and excitement of the real experience of *now* in everyday life. When we face things as they are, we give up the hope of something better. There will be no magic, because we cannot tell ourselves to get out of our depression. Depression and ignorance, the emotions, whatever we experience, are all real and contain tremendous truth. If we really want to learn and see the experience of truth, we have to be where we are. The whole thing is just a matter of being a grain of sand.

At the same time we really have not, I believe, to be afraid of claiming spiritual power from and for God because the world at this stage is in desperate need of it. In the same way that romantic love has to turn into workaday love, and steady commitment in the ordinary, sticking it out through fair weather and foul—so the aspect of glimpsing the glory has to be seen as the opening of a gateway in human awareness, so that going through it, spiritual maturity can proceed in quite a mundane way. The heart of the process surely is that increasingly we know ourselves as an organic part of the kingdom of heaven penetrating earth, so that in our life and death we enter more consciously into the stream of eternal meaning.

\*　　\*　　\*

Hiroshima changed everything. By splitting the atom, men mastered the key to matter and gained an ability to destroy the world. This led the divine to bring forth a spiritual answer from within humanity.

The other day I found jottings I made twenty-five years ago on this subject, taken from the Russian Orthodox writer, Nicholas Berdyaev:[56]

Human nature may contract or expand. Or rather human nature is rooted in infinity and has access to boundless energy. But man's consciousness may be narrowed down and repressed. Just as the atom contains enormous and terrible force which can only be released by splitting the atom (the secret of it has not yet been discovered) so the human monad contains enormous and terrible force which can be released by melting down consciousness and removing its limits. Insofar as human nature is narrowed down by consciousness, it becomes shallow and unreceptive. It feels cut off from the sources of creative energy. What makes a man interesting and significant is that his mind has so to speak an opening into infinity. But average normal consciousness tries to close this opening and then man finds it difficult to manifest all his gifts and resources of creative energy.

Above all, human love and sex have to be harnessed to the spiritual, as has always been known in the mystical tradition. In modern times, Teilhard de Chardin spoke out on the subject:

The day will come, when, after harnessing the ether, the winds, the tides, gravitation, we shall harness for God the energies of love, and on that day, for the second time, in the history of the world, man will have discovered Fire.[57]

A foretaste of the extraordinary power to be released, is shown in the life of Jesus, when he walked on the sea, fed a concourse of people from a handful of food, turned water into wine, miraculously healed the sick, and raised the dead. These may seem to be distant perspectives, but by glimpsing them we hasten their coming. My own journey, however, has happened very slowly and over long quiet years, with very occasional breakthroughs about every seventh year.

**Learning through Buddhism**
Like going back to school, from time to time I have sought and found special help in the next stage of growth, as when at the beginning of the 70s (while continuing to attend Friends

151

regularly) I began to go to Theravada Buddhist retreats. This I did five times for a week at a time over six monthly intervals.

Theravada is the type of Buddhism most akin to Quakers, having no set forms of ritual or symbols. 'Insight Meditation'[58] requires no teaching, though to watch one's breath is the recognized way to enter the meditative state. Dhirawamsa, a Thai monk, was in charge of the small retreat house where I stayed and the day's timetable was rigorous.

At 5.30 till 7.0 each morning and again from 7.0 till 8.30 each evening, the four or five retreatants joined the master in a semi-darkened quiet room, in which stood a small statue of the Buddha, lit with a candle. Here one had to remain motionless in meditation, using a small kneeling stool. Meals were taken corporately, and after breakfast everyone visited the master for about five minutes, in order to let him know how things were going. Speech, reading or writing were not otherwise allowed. It was explained at the outset that the point was so to quieten the mind as to be able to watch one's thoughts as they arose, if possible seeing what brought them to the surface, how they tried to impose themselves as desire and how, when resisted, they finally died away or gave place to another desire. This certainly is not prayer, but it is tough discipline! I suffered acute attacks of boredom, and I still remember how guilty I felt in watching the delightful grey squirrels running up and down the fir trees in the garden outside my window, and when I sneakily allowed myself a half hour's read before sleep. Fortunately I was allowed more than the usual quota of a twenty-minute walk, because having an active dog at home, I was used to so much more exercise than most people.

Two things I remember in particular from the conversations with the master. The first happened in about the third visit, when he searched me with questions—'You have never yet had a breakdown of emotion here: most people weep and despair as they enter further into themselves, and you seem

152

without any such symptoms; I wonder if you are in fact meditating properly?' I told him that as a Quaker I had steadily practised inner silence for many years, usually having about an hour's quiet in the morning, and had at one time suffered an appalling breakthrough in which all the past rose up to be owned and dealt with. Perhaps, I suggested, the gradual Quaker approach, taken seriously, is a much gentler and more natural way of releasing the inner darkness, bringing about the kind of analysis a good psychiatrist might induce through the study of dreams. He nodded and agreed that it might well be so.

Again on the fourth retreat, I remember having a vision of the Transcendental which came to me as *the Light of Love*. When I reported this to Dhirawamsa, he remarked that to see this as *Love* was a very Christian experience, and seldom happened to Thailand meditators, who see it as *Light*.

I could not help wickedly recalling William Blake's rhyme:

> To those who dwell in realms of night
> God doth appear and God is Light.
> To those who dwell in realms of day,
> He doth a *human form* display.

However the deepest value of Buddhist meditation for me was in discovering many things about myself as a human/spiritual machine. I learnt eventually how to watch my body moving and to surprise it in the act of wanting to get up and go, or my eye in the act of seeing, and so on. I saw I *was* in an odd way the machine and yet I wasn't because *I* (whatever *I* was) was watching it. Also *I* didn't seem to be my emotions because these flowed on regardlessly like tides. Again *I* wasn't my own inner self because I could not govern it. In fact (hideous moment!) *I* wasn't anything at all. But that clearly made nonsense because *here I am*. The old Buddhist conundrum discovered as my own.

This train of experience used to continue its momentum

after I returned home, so that gradually over the months I came to the conclusion that it was true *I was nothing*. That is I was akin to worms, mud, clouds, and I remember ruefully stroking the earth, rubbing my nose on a leaf, and feeling my dog's warm face against mine—and saying the equivalent of 'Okay, you are only things too, I'll be a thing like you—why not? All flesh is grass, how beautiful to be like grass!' Then I found I had entered into *the thingness of the world* and began to know it as spiritually alive in a very ordinary, *unpeak*-experience-way, more like patting a horse, cuddling a child, touching the sprouting peas, gazing into a crystal, than any spiritual glory. This led on to telling myself 'Who wants spiritual experience, when everything everywhere is spiritual, and spiritual is *nothing*—it's just so ordinary!'

*　　　*　　　*

I came to understand very much more about the hidden treasures of Buddhism from Pir Vilayat Inayat Khan[59] during the three times I attended his Sufi summer camps in the French Alps. These camps are held in tents at six or seven thousand feet. Part of the Pir's teaching is on the meditative experiences of the great faiths of East and West which he gives against the background of a disciplined silence. His rich spiritual presence provided me with the kernel of some of the truths I had already been glimpsing in meditation and he pointed the way in which the great traditions may be seen to complement each other.

We were encouraged to practise (over a three-week period) Hindu, Buddhist and Christian mystical practices, while hearing what fruit they were likely to bear. The central Hindu practice of a mantra (which I knew at first-hand through Transcendental Meditation) should lead one towards *Samadhi*, where personal thought disappears in the silence of eternity, but Buddhism carries one a step further still.

The Buddha had enquired how Samadhi (entering into the spiritual void within) was going to save the world and why the Yoga Schools of his time concentrated on the Siddhis (the exciting psychic possibilities which commonly accompany meditation), rather than spiritually relating to man's suffering and dying. He left his father's palace and an easy life in order to experience the pain of the world. After many years, having followed the life of a renunciate, under the Bodhi tree where he had sat for weeks, he leaped up shouting 'The Way has been found!'

This awakening of the Buddha is an awakening from the personal perspective into the discovery that real being is totally impersonal and cosmic. We have all been caught in a manic way of living and dis-identification is the key to escape from the suffering to which we are all subject.

Objectivity is the opposite of subjectivity, and this spectator-aspect of ourselves refuses to identify with our vehicle. From this refusal comes the realization that we are funnels—one end unlimited and eternal, and the other a tiny point which is *us*. We are, as it were, small shoots with an infinite root that intertwines with all life. But the *Satipani* path of Buddhism can carry one to extremes, since its ideal is escape from the world. It is the desirelessness of the recluse, rather than the everyday fulfilment of becoming what you might be. Illumination of that sort then is not so much freedom in and through being fully engaged in living, as entering a higher state of luminous intelligence which is flowing into the world and is (behind the scenes) its source of life.

Buddha saw the whole past, not only of this universe, but also of past universes. He experienced all the planes of being, celestial as well as natural, and communicated with them. This part of Buddhism (so the Pir said) is seldom taught, though Tibetans speak of communication with the demonic and angelic planes—and for this one has to encounter the angelic and demonic aspects of oneself (which are not *unreal* or

155

simply psychotic episodes—as I have reason to know!). Again, the Buddha speaks of the pure splendour and intelligence in which dwell the Great Spiritual Powers from which all things pour forth into existence. Among these are *the Archetypes*, the templates which are the programming power behind the creatures. To be given teaching about them was marvellous, as I had twice (once in a Friends Meeting) glimpsed these Great Forms, which appeared to me more real than the forms in our world.

For Buddhism (as perhaps also for Quakers!) the highest ecstasy is—*Sobriety*. So in one sense Buddhism (like Science) is *cold*; very different from the passionate warmth of Christ. Though in some of its traditions there is the path of the Boddhisatva, the one who has glimpsed paradise beyond suffering, and then renounces it in order to serve and suffer on until the last creature has reached its fulfilment.

**The Cosmic Christ**
Love means involvement and this is the Christian way. Prayer aims at so opening ourselves to the divine that we may become its sons and daughters, and so discover that there is 'One who loves me—and so I have power to love!' The Incarnation then betokens the miracle of the birth of the divine in human consciousness.

C. G. Jung had the daring to say that he found the Christ Archetype in the depth of the human psyche. The astonishing verification of this has been the experience of many. When at the world's end, on the rocks, one is faced with the likelihood of disintegration of being, waiting for the blow to fall, opening one's life to Christ may turn this into a holy undoing by which one is remade at depth.

The heart of the Christian Gospel is that what has been maturing for aeons of time in nature comes to fulfilment in the divine element in us. The universe gradually more and more takes on the countenance of God and we participate in this miracle, attaining to it at the price of all we possess. That is in the agony of the sensitive, the courage of the hungry who dare to share their food, and the overcoming in selfless heroism of the despair of those who enter into spiritual night. In fact the surrender on the cross leading to a breakthrough of the divine.

God is working within humanity to transform things—and this is the work of the Cosmic Christ. Christ in us is the Light that flows from the centre of all Light—to be found in the alcoholic vagrant on the park bench and the one crucified by agonizing illness, as well as in those who triumph. Christ suffers and rejoices in us because *we are him*, though limited by the thought of what we think we are. Naturally our faults are forgiven since we are only half-made beings and on the threshold of a world as yet just beginning to take shape. The Christian path lies in taking responsibility, of accepting the blame, a way of conscience rather than emphasis on the search for increase in consciousness like the Buddhist one. It lies in allowing oneself to appreciate the gulf between us and the pure being of God, and at the same time in realizing we are called to be sons and daughters who begin to allow the reality at the heart of existence to have its way with us.

Entering the consciousness of God in his universe is *not* Samadhi or the Holy Void, rather it is an *encounter with God* —and not only in the quiet of prayer (though that too), but in the poor, the wicked, the stupid, the hungry, in politics, in the peace movement—and most difficult of all, in our own sin and shortcoming. In fact the encounter takes place in the daily vocation of discovering what it is to be human.

*Relationship* is the new thing that Christianity offers to Eastern spirituality, and it is complementary rather than con- tradictory to the Samadhi of Hinduism and the marvellous inner purifications and journeyings of Buddhism. It is the way that chooses to go beyond, by means of suffering love, and this leads to viewing all that happens as precious and important— and in no sense as illusion (*Samsara*).

157

Both East and West have to move towards the knowledge that life *is* indeed part of the being of God, and every individual conscious awareness is aware, not just for itself, but as a point of earth-awareness and God-awareness.

It is not possible to pray to oneself, and in fact the little self can only give the orders and then let go into the beyond of eternity. As Christians express it: 'Not I live now, but Christ lives in me'. In fact we are cells in an *Incredible Live Being* held together in all its parts from human affection down the scale to the nucleus of the atom—by Love. The whole work of the world—human, animal, plant and crystal, the movement of the seas and the force of all the energies—are then (if we could only experience it!) *Love made manifest.* This is not just hyperbole—it may be spiritually known, as the mystics have taught down the years in all traditions.

This faith sends people out into the task of taking on world karma, that is the suffering hurt laid upon our generation from the past, engaging alongside the divine in the day-to-day purposing of history. There really is an inner nudging towards consciousness, a divine lure towards feeling.[60] This is not so much an accident as *a purposing* which derives from millions of coincidences which finally have brought out of blind chaos, first life, then awareness, and which in the end moves towards divine awareness. The experiment may not succeed on this small planet of a small sun, in a minor galaxy, but who knows what other experiments are happening in the hundreds of galaxies away in space?

By our inner verification we know that we are in some sense an experiment in which there has been a tremendous investment by nature, perhaps the greatest investment that has been made anywhere in all the universes. Who knows too that what might well look like utter failure and destruction to us, in our limited ability to comprehend, may turn out to be a divine success?

In going forward into New Paradigm thinking I understand

the *Cross* and *Resurrection* as an underlying pattern, with grace like a blood-transfusion connecting man's technical success with power to become more warmly human in our ability to weave at depth with nature. Jesus for me demonstrates what the divine looks like when it flows in man unimpeded.

I agree with John Yungblut[61] that it blocks me to say to myself *Jesus is God* and it opens me to say, *Jesus, as the Christ of God*, was the Forerunner of many in whom the divine has become conscious. The divine in humanity I believe to be the Cosmic Christ revealing himself in his Second Coming, and it is to his spirit (shown us in the life, death and resurrection of Jesus) that we need to try to open ourselves. The Holy Spirit may inwardly be known as conscience and inner guide, through whom we are made conscious of being fused into a living unity with all else: the microcosm of the macrocosm. At the other polarity, as disciples we are able to say that homely thing *Abba, Father*, discovering that life reaches us as an incredible Guru, who does not flinch from delivering us the severest disciplines, if it is this that will break through the inner defences by which we thrust off the inner guidance of the divine.

In an era like ours where science dominates the Western psyche, for many the Christian symbols no longer resonate, and forms of meditation rather than the sacraments of the churches are an easier step into spiritual reality. Meditation may lead to the coolness of right self-appraisal and recognition of our own compulsions, bringing a direct experience of the inner light, and a fresh falling in love with goodness and truth. It does seem as though our archetypes require new symbols and that the spiritual power is being withdrawn from those which have come down to us from the past.

*I personally believe that there is a quality in the bareness of Christian Quakerism, which may act as a bridge between the past and the future, allowing space for Friends to dare to search within.*

At the same time we must recognize that the insights of modern psychology indicate that man's deeper movements within, which relate him to his own subconscious and also to the mysterious worlds in which he finds himself, work by means of myth, ritual and symbol. Religion is not only a private exploration; it belongs also to the whole substance of life in process of evolution.

I grew up steeped in the Catholic tradition (I was brought up Anglo-Catholic) and the old way has a hold upon me still. I became a Quaker because I found the Communion at church altars so claustrophobic that years would go by without my being able to take it. The vision I glimpsed could not be contained in so small a compass, and like George Fox, I felt churches hid Christ rather than revealed the fact that all life is sacramental. Most of the time, I feel this still.

It is terrifying as well as beautiful to glimpse that we eat the body and blood of God in daily bread, either to our destruction or our salvation. All the world is doing exactly what this symbolizes, and the crucifixion and resurrection process lies in the way in which it is done. As we act towards the littlest and least, we do it also to the divine component within it, and that goes for forests, for whales, for the earth's atmosphere and for every other man, woman and child on earth.

It is curious to find that I have been travelling towards this position all my life. My first pamphlet written in 1954 contained this passage:

> We have to embrace reality in every way that it offers itself to us, to seek the source of it, to find it threaded through the world, to bring it to the surface if we can, to bring it out of hiding and incarnate it. I am sure this is what Jesus meant. He was the most living person there has ever been. A force of life rings through his actions and words that come out of reality itself, out of the very heart of God. In his words we come face to face with what is real; in him, time and eternity met fully for the first

160

time, and his life and power are altogether beyond this world. It is knowledge of overpowering life that makes real any message about death.[62]

I have come then into a new mode of being a Christian and a Quaker, because I find I can joyfully and with security include all my spiritual experience gathered on a life's journey. I am not so much a Universalist in approach as someone who, receiving plenteously from the East, is able to offer back the enriched gift of my own Christian heritage (enriched by Jungian and Teilhardian thought). To be a Quaker is by no means to say goodbye to myth, ritual and symbol, but rather to find myself set free to discover them as the very essence of the way I now experience, so that my ethics become mystical ethics and my life and death reach out to me as sacraments.

I end feeling as did G. K. Chesterton: that as his voyage's end was in sight, he found that as his ship drew near the coast, it turned out to be the white cliffs of Dover.

*Now my book would have ended here but for a strange inward journey, the diary of which is now appended. Some of my readers may be inclined to attribute it to the fact of the hysterectomy I had to undergo, since this is well known to cause turmoil in the emotional life—and there is a sense in which they would be right. Others, however, may take the line which I take myself, that God down through history has approached his servants by means of great dreams, and that through suffering inward doors may open.*

*I believe too that there is a certain type of dream which belongs not only to the dreamer, but also to his friends and his culture, and declares hidden truth which it is difficult to express in terms to which reason can listen.*

# CHAPTER 7

## DIARY OF AN INWARD JOURNEY

Back in June 1983 I began to feel I needed to undertake some inner work and plucked up courage to write to E.H. (a Jungian analyst and a priest who is a great friend and helper of a friend of mine). I asked him to glance through my Swarthmore Lecture so that he could see the kind of person I was, and then, if he would be kind enough, to advise me how to set about this.

I had no reply until September, but because the matter was important I made no effort to follow up my first approach, leaving life itself to decide whether contact should be made.

Finally he got in touch with me, saying he had read my book while on holiday and would be glad to meet me. I visited him and he agreed to see me regularly for about three months so that we could then discover where this led.

I feared I might be unable to remember my dreams as he suggested that I try to do, but in the first night's trial I was overtaken by what appeared to me as a powerful and inexplicable spiritual event. As I woke in the middle of the night in the twilight area of half-sleep, a voice said to me: 'Are you willing to be subject to the message of the Dark Guardian and his secret?' Whereupon my inward self immediately replied: 'Only under Christ and his sign for the redemption of the world'. This oracular mode is so unlike my natural one that I regarded it with awe!

I visited E.H. again early in October and shared with him what had happened. He suggested I might try to see if I could enter into myself and draw near to the Dark Guardian. On doing this I immediately saw a giant Mexican-type stone figure (square mouth, square eyes) which reached up to the dark sky and blocked an attractive valley; a fast flowing river ran between its legs towards me. I shared this with E.H. and he suggested that I question it as to its message and its secret, and on my doing this it turned its back on me and as I watched, the figure became surrounded with light so that the details disappeared, and at the same time the river between its legs rose into a mighty flood and engulfed me. As I saw that I should drown, I found myself in a small boat, and this, despite the rush of the powerful waters, travelled against the flow, through the giant legs and came to rest in a sunlit valley. Looking up I saw that the figure had become the Cosmic Christ resplendent with light, alive and shining in a holy glory.

E.H. interpreted the flood waters as the rise of the unconscious, the stone figure as the deadness within me that blocked the waters of life, and he thought that the small boat, appearing from nowhere to save me, was Christ.

I could not relate well to his interpretation, but had a strong sense that life was about to lead me into something which at present I could not guess. I said, 'Perhaps I shall go mad or become ill or something'. 'Do you expect that?' E.H. asked, and laughing I replied, 'No such thing: Though I am visiting the doctor for the first time for years with a mild urinary trouble'.

Within a couple of days the doctor had told me that I had a large tumour of some kind which would have to be removed. I refused an urgent appointment with a specialist, as Frederick was due to take the last Fungus Week of his life at Nettlecombe Field Study Centre near Minehead. With the hilly country to be traversed and the exhausting time he would have, I felt my first commitment lay there. We had a beautiful week, and two days before the end of it I had another visionary dream.

This time it was of a vortex of huge energy and power down which I was fatally attracted, while at the same time being aware that if I should be drawn into it I would be whirled into an abyss which betokened my end. As I returned to the surface, in the twilight area on the edge of dream, it was made known to me that it was this abyss to which mankind was at present being fatally attracted and it was necessary for some of us to enter it in full spiritual awareness, because only so could healing be mediated to the world.

Two days after my return from Nettlecombe I had an appointment with the surgeon, who told me that I had a tumour the size of a grapefruit on an ovary, and this would have to be removed. If it proved to be benign then the operation would simply remove it; if it was malignant, then a hysterectomy would have to be done and both ovaries removed. I warned Frederick that in view of the inner warnings I had received, it was almost certain that it was malignant. This proved to be the case.

However, it was something of a shock on the day after the operation to hear from the surgeon that he had removed a large cancerous tumour and also found some grainy cancer of a different type in the rectum. I realized I would be unlikely to live long. I also knew for certain that I was embarking on the most important inward journey of my life and nothing was happening by accident.

Following the operation all sense of God disappeared, and anyone who came to my bedside (and the love and visiting I received was one of the great treasures of my life) I asked to take my hand and mediate God's love to me. In fact healing and prayer surrounded me on every hand, although I myself felt cut off in complete inner aridity except when actually held in the inner place by someone taking my hand and praying. I had to suffer a good deal physically too—something I had not done except in childbirth. This was due not only to the severity of the operation (the surgeon said, 'We really had to butcher you about'), but also the blood-clotting in the area of the operation. When people tell me that now in modern medicine most suffering may be prevented, I know this is untrue.

As I lay in hospital I had a burning need to return to my childhood patterns and asked that D.B. (the vicar of the next village whose wife I have been visiting weekly for some years when we pray for people together) should bring me the Holy Communion. This he did, and in my state of complete inability to know the inner light, I found it literally the Bread of Life to me. I held on inwardly by means of it and knew the presence of Christ was within, even though I could sense nothing.

Alongside this I began to acknowledge my bitter contamination of life. This became worse and worse until I needed to confess, particularly one hidden thing from long ago.

This had happened 43 years ago when as a young mother, my third baby due two days later, in the middle of the night after hours of cuddling and loving my ill two-year-old, suddenly coming to breaking-point at his continued crying, I had hurt him. No physical damage was done, but I have never forgotten the look on my darling's face. Yes, I cuddled him once again, crying with pain myself, and then returning him to his cot, he fell fast asleep. In fact, in the morning it was discovered that he had had a blockage very low down in the bowel, which had passed of its own accord, and it was amazing that he had survived the night. All this came back to me as though it was happening now and I managed to tell the whole story to a Friend whom I love and trust, weeping my heart out as I did so. She said, 'You were forgiven *as* it happened' and this was precious but I found my heart was not set at rest. I had failed long ago because of inherent insufficiency, and I understood more and more as the days passed that my whole life was tarred with the brush of not having loved enough.

Now from eight years old until I left the church when I was twenty, I had made my confession to a priest regularly. Indeed it was one of the enormous reliefs of my life that I escaped from this soul-searching when I became a communist.

166

Now I went back to that early pattern. What I had received from my Friend I knew to be true, but I could not inwardly take hold of it. I knew I needed to re-experience the old way, with a ritual of penitance, and so I wrote to E.H. in his priestly capacity, asking him if he would now act as my spiritual director and hear my confession. I had only been a day or two out of hospital and was weak physically, emotionally and spiritually when he came. We talked and I laid bare my heart. He was wonderfully helpful in leading me to accept myself and what had happened long ago—and in the most practical way too. He added that it was necessary to understand at depth that everything we do has its shadow side, and there is nothing which in fact is pure. This I was desperately experiencing, and it was a gift to have my inward tune played back to me. I then confessed formally and received absolution. After that the weight was lifted.

A day or two later Frederick and I went to Burrswood, the Dorothy Kerin Healing Home, to convalesce for a fortnight. Here I made my communion daily. I wrote in my diary:

> I now see that E.H. was right when he said the small boat was Jesus Christ in the visionary experience I had when with him. I have to realize that my spiritual desire of many years to understand more deeply the meaning of Christ is being answered.

I understood freshly first that Jesus is a human personality fully illumined by the divine, a person who may be known as people know people; second, he is the Christ of God who is the Word spoken into Creation from the beginning.

Previously I had experienced the Cosmic aspect, and now I was being approached by the human one. Father Keith Donnerly at Burrswood suggested further that I should seek to experience Christ in his *resurrected aspect* and only experience the suffering of the world in and through this. Writing this book I saw I had entered into the suffering of the world more deeply than I had realized, night after night lying awake trying to pray for its salvation.

Returning home and to my beloved Friends Meeting, I realized more fully the awkwardness of needing now to make my communion each week. However, this I began to do in the village church, hardly understanding what drove me to need it and suspecting it was a regression back to childhood which possibly did not have the validity of maturity. However, the inner command was strong and I felt I must obey it—I have continued to do so ever since.

At Burrswood I had received healing both at services and in my room with anointing from Father Donnerley. Also my dear Quaker friends Jim and Beryl Pym visited me and gave me healing. They all knew I did not want any healing that did not relate to the deep vocation that was exercising itself in me and which might entail my dying. The blessing I received through them seemed to pinpoint all the love, healing and prayers of very many people who loved me and whom I knew were praying for me. Whether for life or death I felt (still do!) surrounded by caring.

Twice during my time in hospital when things were at their worst (despite the fact that my spiritual-psychic senses were blacked out, due, I was later told, to the anaesthetic) I received what I can only describe as a spiritual hug. The second time it happened, I realized it came from Sister Margaret Theresa, the old head of my Anglican convent (Wantage) school when I was a girl—now dead for many years.

Just before Christmas I visited E.H. again. It was reassuring to be able to say out loud how precious it was to find myself at unity with all people and all denominations who seek to understand the Incarnation process. This was not only in my village church where I was attending early on Sunday morning, but also Brethren, Catholics—yes, Evangelicals of all kinds, Jesus Freaks. All from the apparently most primitive to my own beloved Quakers with our austere bareness of approach. I said I needed to receive the Sacrament just because it has been valid for people in extremity and in community all down the ages since the beginning. I needed to hear it spoken aloud 'through Him we offer thee our souls, and bodies as a living sacrifice'. I needed to hear 'Holy, Holy, Holy' spoken aloud by ordinary people like myself—as the assertion of the other dimension.

On December 22nd I felt drawn back to taking another look at my old paintings of the Suffering Christ. I had done these at Pendle Hill after the Easter Retreat with Parker and Sally Palmer in 1976, and they came as an outpouring from great depth. Then once I had painted them, my recurrent nightmares connected with seeing people badly beaten up in the Night Shelter disappeared. It was as though something in me beyond reason understood there was an eternal echo in this happening and all such terrible happenings.

I took out the paintings (which I know by heart in every line anyway) and pondering began to feel profound awe and fear. My own physical and emotional extremity now required the same archetypal image. It came to me that while I identified with the pictures, at the same time I knew that in some sense Christ's passion was happening *in my place*—and this is part of what the redemption means. This shook me to the core in its terror and beauty and I longed to cry and cry and cry. However, that had to happen inwardly and not actually, because Christmas was upon me, the young people and grandchildren coming down, mince pies to make and so on. Fortunately a part of me remained quite serene.

This was a psychic/spiritual thing I glimpsed: namely, that a certain dark something we do not have to bear, because it is possible to be hid with Christ in God: 'In all our afflictions he is made to suffer' and from this rivers of peace and purification continually flow.

All the same I felt desperation. I dreamed of being a miner, with a pick at the coal-face, black and struggling in the dark, because fresh supplies of coal had to be got. My crisis arose from understanding that Love interpenetrates all man's suffering and the strange fact that though we have to go into the dark vortex where personality disintegrates, yet 'all is well' because of Christ in us—but the divine does this at appalling cost.

In this state although surrounded by dear ones, I felt utterly lonely. I sent off my old paintings to E.H. because I wanted to distance myself from them. In fact I wrote hectically four days running, wishing I could prevent myself. I needed the company of someone whom I knew for certain traverses from time to time the great spaces within. There was no reply. In fact he was away skiing, but of this I had no idea. I had to come to terms with this silence, telling myself that unavailability of a person was not necessarily rejection. I was clear too that I had not chosen E.H. as my helper—he had been given me. If therefore he did not reply this was because it had to be so.

My awe (and terror even) at being alone with the Great Forms from which life issues only happened *when I was not actually experiencing them.* It came when I returned and began to question myself about what had been happening.

Then I had a dream about someone who 25 years ago I had inwardly accompanied during his dying and for three days after his death—although I was at a distance and in fact quite busy at the time. This was authenticated for me by the fact that in semi-consciousness as he was dying he kept repeating my name. I now realized that if it was possible for me to do that for someone, how much more was it not possible for E.H. to do the same for me—since I felt his commitment to me. From then on I plugged into his spiritual warmth and strength and my fear died away.

I had another gift too in the shape of having an impulse to take down Berdyaev's *Destiny of Man*[63] and opening it I found a passage that came like a caress from a wise friend:

170

And therefore we must paradoxically think of the end of the world both as in time and in eternity. The end of the world, like the end of each individual man, is an event both immanent and transcendent. Horror and anguish are caused by this incomprehensible combination of the transcendent with the immanent, the temporal and the eternal. For every one of us and for the world as a whole there comes a catastrophe, a jump across the abyss, a mysterious escape from time which takes place in time. The death of the individual is also a deliverance from time taking place in time. . . . Eternal life is revealed in time, it may unfold itself in every instant as an eternal present. Eternal life is not a future life but life in the present, life in the depths of an instant of time. In those depths time is torn asunder. It is therefore a mistake to expect eternity in the future in an existence beyond the grave and to look forward to death in time in order to enter into the divine life. Strictly speaking eternity will never come in the future—in the future there can only be bad infinity. Only hell can be thought of in this way. Eternity and eternal life come not in the future but in a moment, i.e. they are deliverance from time, and mean ceasing to project life into time.

What was happening to me now was a practice in acceptance of the loneliness we know before God and our own death.

At this point then, just after Christmas, the whole rhythm of my life suddenly changed. From being a semi-invalid just finishing convalescence, I began once again to be called upon for help from those to whom I was committed. One of those on my overseers' list had a serious stroke, another who was taking his Ph.D. went into hospital and needed a daily visit to support him through ECT treatment. A neighbour across the road who used long ago to suffer mental trouble now needed a daily visit of support. A number of beloved young people were in Cambridge for Christmas and came to see me, and we had deep exchanges. In this way the sense that more spiritual energy was passing through me than I could easily bear passed, and I felt able to pass on the healing and love that had been flowing to me from so many.

At the Christmas midnight mass it came to me that I now was beginning to understand *why* I needed communion at the altar. This was to bring 'my body to be made clean by His body and my soul washed through His most precious blood'. In doing this I discovered a new way to pray—first bringing myself into the holy presence, then the body of all the people on earth and all life too (which I knew in a fresh way as *my* body) and finally the body of the planet as it hangs in blue space. I understood too that it was hard to be personally cleansed of my own body's pollution while my larger body (which is other people and the earth) remains polluted.

This became then something that was happening in and through me. I understood that a spiritual kind of 'operation' and had been going on as well as the physical one in hospital. It was like a fairytale event. I had had to obey what the oracle spoke—to do something that appeared to me unreasonable; only then could my heart's desire be realized.

I had done the unreasonable things in obedience: I had howled aloud for my sins, I had made my confession, I had returned to the communion service to receive symbolically the body and blood of Christ. Out of this I had received a grace. I had cried, 'I have never loved enough', and now my heart had in a strange way been opened up to *love more*. This was not something I could have achieved for myself, since I could not in the least envisage what it would be like.

Soon after understanding this, I received another visionary dream, which has brought me to a further lodging place.

I dreamed I was with a small group of people whom I knew and loved and we were together lifting something up for the angels to deal with. As I came to the surface of wakefulness, a voice said to me: 'Remember the Guardian'. I drowsily thought 'Guardian? Guardian? Is it the newspaper?' and then with a shock realized this was my inner Guardian. I then asked what it was that we were lifting up for the angels to deal with. The reply came: 'All who are in trouble, sorrow, need, sickness or any other adversity. You are learning obedience, and what is happening to you, you yourself utterly require.' Next I had a vision of the round world with all its agonized suffering of mind, body and soul and felt part of it, and at the side of this as a vignette, was a picture of a very vital woman (Indian, I think) with hennaed hair, writhing in bodily pain and spiritual extremity. Then the voice went on: 'This could take you and squeeze you until your body dies, aren't you afraid?' I replied 'Yes, I *am* afraid!' whereupon I heard in great power: 'Fear not, it is I!' My fear then immediately left me and I felt an ecstasy of joy. I then scribbled down what had happened and fell asleep again. As I woke in the morning I was aware I had been somewhere spiritual and I found my mind searching for all its praise words: 'Thou art the Beautiful, Thou art the Faithful, Thou art the Beloved, Thou art the Holy One, Thou art the First Born of Every Creature!'

From this point, I knew that I was in some way identified with the world's divine transmutation, and nothing will ever happen to me by accident. Lately I have felt as if I were living in the present moment as never before. I go to the hospital monthly and am on chemotherapy, and so far (11 months) have had no recurrence of my cancer. It turns out to be extraordinarily satisfying to be receiving life from God at short term.

Abundance of life has been given me and I find assurance of purpose and laughter within myself. My husband and I have never been so happy together I think. The groups of people with whom I am closely connected seem to me brimming over with shared spiritual life; the veil between us and the 'people up there' is thin. I am certain they and we are working together far more as a network than we generally suppose, and this is the meaning of 'the communion of saints'.

As the months go by I am certainly *less* spiritually psychic, and I am only too aware that this is a lodging place only. Nothing in nature stands still, least of all one's bodily, mental and spiritual condition. If I fall ill again, or lose all sense of the nearness of the spirit, perhaps I shall grow frightened or lose my nerve. However, taking up my paintbrush once again after a long lapse, I found myself engaged in a further series of pictures of the Suffering Christ—but this time Jesus had beside him—*a woman.* I knew this woman *as all of us.*

E.H. with whom I have continued taking counsel once a month during all this time, told me he believed (though he had no firm evidence) that often cancer came as the result of a need for growth. 'You have had a breakthrough on a scale which perhaps may mean that you have no need now to die of cancer.' This could be so. I have had two more Guardian dreams which imply something of the kind, though both suggest not too long postponed a departure.

The first which I had some months ago has a punning quality. In it I found I was walking with the Guardian in the local nature reserve (where I walk most days) and he said to me *'You have been given a doubling of your life energies in order that you may walk to the end of your nature reserve'.* I walked on, binoculars as usual round my neck, and at the far end, which came more quickly than I anticipated, I found a sky-high and horizon-wide, patterned barrier. I questioned myself whether the patterning was a coat of arms, or a huge Chinese character, and then it came to me that it was a mystical sign and when I passed through it, then I should be able to comprehend the pattern.

The second dream I had quite recently and this time before going to sleep I requested the Guardian to speak to me about my life and death. In it I found myself with two angel companions setting out on a journey which I understood had now

174

been doubled in length. Away in the dark of the far distance I saw a ruined castle on the edge of the sea, and knew this for my final destination. Although the angels had fine upstanding wings like the sails of yachts, I had an intimation that they were broken. As I came to the surface of wakefulness, I asked the Guardian to tell me who the angels were and why they had broken wings. He replied 'They are the angels of your being and their wings are not really broken, but this is fortunate for you, it means they cannot fly away, but will now stay on as your companions. When you reach the sea, you will fly with them'.

When I attempted to paint the Angel Dream I discovered that the two angels were the Angel of Death and the Angel of Life, and each time I tried, I discovered myself as a teenager hand in hand with them. In fact we all walk hand in hand with Death and Life and must own to a child within.

I was able blessedly to pick up the threads of my life very quickly after my illness, the two committees of which I am secretary did not miss my presence for even a single meeting. One joy was that the University of the Third Age group I had been teaching on Teilhard de Chardin, had the courage to carry on without me while I was ill, and then the kindness to allow me on my return in the Easter term to lead them through the chapters of this book.

Soon after Christmas my husband and I began to make plans, meaning to use what time we had left, profitably. We booked in, and were able to enjoy, in June a holiday with old friends in Scotland, which included a bird-watching week on Mull. This was followed by a seminar held by the Scientific and Medical Network on Iona organized by our Quaker Friends Douglas and Carola Mathers. This was a precious time and I was given more healing by Gordon Barker while I was there.

Despite the risk of my being unable to come, when I wrote in January to my friends at Viitakivi International Centre in

Finland, offering myself as a lecturer in the August seminar, I was accepted. This was my sixth visit there, and the joy of seeing everyone again was great. I also had a quickie trip to Saarijarvi Yoga centre to give a lecture on 'Spirituality East and West: Complementary or Contradictory?' and then a weekend at Lappeenranta, near the Soviet border to visit a healing group.

On my return, our family and grandchildren spent a few days together by the sea, using the Wells-next-the-Sea Friends Meeting house holiday flat. Then returning home for twenty-four hours, Frederick (who had just completed one more mathematics book) took off for Brittany with the Council of Field Studies in a minibus.

I have a busy programme between now and Christmas, which includes giving talks or taking retreats away from home about once a fortnight. Also I visit two cancer patients weekly and we share and do meditation together.

*The Gentle Way With Cancer* method suggests actual picturing of the cancer itself as a physical entity and then imagining its cleansing, with the white corpuscles destroying the weaker cancer cells. For me the curative base has been the repetition several times a day of the words: 'My body is being made clean by Thy Body, and my soul washed through Thy most precious Blood'. I am aware too in my quiet morning hour, and as I practise T'ai Chi, that I am opening myself in every cell to the healing and wholeness of divine energies within. At the same time, I feel quite friendly towards my departure into the next world. In the earlier months after the operation, I often felt as though part of me was already taking off there, and when the time comes I suspect I shall hear the call. Death is surely an initiation of the greatest power, and has to be looked forward to in that way. If it turns out painful, this might well be because something in me requires to experience this for love's sake and on the world's behalf. Meanwhile I have never felt better in my life and a recent hospital scan gave me a clean sheet.

I certainly would not have missed the cancer experience, since these past months have been the most valuable of my life. Part of this has been due to the realization that what I had written in some chapters of this book, I am now in a much deeper way, able to know as my own.

It is interesting too, that when I said something of this kind to the doctor who sees me at the cancer clinic, he remarked that he was not at all surprised, adding that perhaps 60% of patients who talk to him, say something like this. 'It is as though cancer may actually bring out the best in people, if they are ready for that to happen. This is not the case, for instance with diabetes clinic patients, where I have never had a comment made to me of this sort.'

This period has brought me full circle back to my spiritual beginnings so that the inner secrets of my childhood are restored as a flowering of my maturity. I now see that for me the sacraments, symbols and myths of churches (of all world religions) express inward truth which can be taken hold of in no other way. They were not invented, they happened, and are the Great Dreams of whole peoples and cultures.

Many of us today find it hard to feel at home in any church and feel ourselves to be strangers and pilgrims on the way. Probably the Society of Friends is a surer home than any other for those of us who are perpetually forced by the logic of our inner lives into further adventuring. This is as it should be, bridges have to be built between the old and the new, and new symbolism will without doubt arise.

*Quakers are bridge people.* I remain on that bridge, part of my roots reaching back into the Christian past, and part stretching forward into the future where new symbols are being born.

In my end is my beginning, and the way out is the way in.

# REFERENCES AND FURTHER READING

[1] Damaris Parker-Rhodes, *Truth: a path and not a possession.* Swarthmore Lecture. London: Friends Home Service Committee, 1977.

[2] *Advices and Queries.* London Yearly Meeting of the Religious Society of Friends, 1964.

[3] Lyall Watson, *Supernature.* London: Coronet Books, 1974, *Lifetide.* London: Coronet Books, 1980, and *The Gift of Unknown Things.* London: Coronet Books, 1977.

[4] Fritjof Capra, *The Tao of Physics.* London: Fontana, 1976, and *The Turning Point.* London: Fontana, 1983.

[5] Marilyn Ferguson, *The Aquarian Conspiracy.* London: Routledge, 1981.

[6] James Lovelock, *Gaia, a new look at Life on Earth.* Oxford University Press, 1979.

[7] Peter Russell, *The Awakening Earth.* Routledge, 1982, p. 9.

[8] Lovelock, *op. cit.*

[9] Pierre Teilhard de Chardin, *The Future of Man.* London: Collins, 1965, *The Phenomenon of Man.* London: Collins, 1960, and *Le Milieu Divin.* London: Collins, 1960.

[10] From *The Human Search with Teilhard de Chardin* ed. by George Appleton. London: Fount, 1979, p. 94.

[11] Russell, *op. cit.*, p. 20.

[12] From 'Epigrams, verses and fragments', written about 1808–11, in *Poetry and Prose of William Blake*, ed. Geoffrey Keynes. London: Nonesuch Library, 4th edn., 1961.

[13] Parker-Rhodes, *op. cit.*

[14] Isaac Penington (1653), quoted in *Christian Faith and Practice in the Experience of the Society of Friends.* London Yearly Meeting, 1960, 'To the reader'.

[15] Jeff Nuttall, *Bomb Culture.* St. Albans: Paladin Books, 1970.

[16] Theodore Roszak, *The Making of a Counter Culture.* London: Faber, 1970, *Where the Wastelands End.* London: Faber, 1972, and *Person Planet.* London: Gollancz, 1979.

[17] From 'Proverbs of Hell' in *Poetry and Prose of William Blake* ed. by Geoffrey Keynes.

[18] Nena and George O'Neill, *Open Marriage: a new life style for couples.* London: Peter Owen, 1973.

[19] Michael Adams, *Wandering in Eden.* New York: Knopf, 1976.

[20] From 'Proverbs of Hell in the Marriage of Heaven and Hell', *Poetry and Prose of William Blake* ed. by Geoffrey Keynes. London: Nonesuch Library, 4th edn., 1961.

[21] Irina Tweedie, *Chasm of Fire*. Salisbury, Wilts: Element Books, 1979.

[22] Elaine Pagels, *The Gnostic Gospels*. New York: Random House, 1979.

[23] *Ibid.*, Introduction, p. xvii.

[24] John Brown in Seekers' Association Papers (Barbara Scott's group on June Singer's *Androgyny: a new theory of sexuality*. Routledge, 1977).

[25] *Ibid.*

[26] C. G. Jung, *Collected Works*, vol. 11 'Answer to Job'. London: Routledge, 1978.

[27] Gandhi, quoted in *Conjectures of a Guilty Bystander* by Thomas Merton. New York: Doubleday, 1968, p. 83.

[28] David Brandon, *The Zen of Helping*. London: Routledge, 1976.

[29] Joanna R. Macy, *Despair and Personal Power in the Nuclear Age*. Philadelphia, USA: New Society Publishers, 1984.

[30] Jim Garrison, *From Hiroshima to Harrisburg*. London: SCM, 1980, and *The Darkness of God: Theology after Hiroshima*. London: SCM, 1982.

[31] T. S. Eliot, *Four Quartets*. London: Faber, 1944.

[32] Thomas Merton, *op. cit.*, p. 68.

[33] Agnes Sandford, *The Healing Light*. Evesham, Worcs: Arthur James, 1972, and *Sealed Order*. Plainfield, NJ, USA: Logos International, 1972.

[34] A. Frederick Parker-Rhodes, *The Theory of Indistinguishables*. Dordrecht, Netherlands: Reidel Publishing, 1981.

[35] Carlos Castenada, *The Teachings of Don Juan*. Harmondsworth, Middx: Penguin Books, 1970.

[36] Martin Israel in *The Christian Parapsychologist* (1982) A quarterly journal of the Churches Fellowship of Psychical and Spiritual Studies.

[37] D. H. Lawrence, 'Shadows' in *Selected Poems*. Harmondsworth, Middx.: Penguin Books, 1972, p. 257.

[38] Teilhard de Chardin, *Le Milieu Divin*, op. cit., p. 118.

[39] *Ibid.*, p. 6.

[40] *Ibid.*, p. 69.

[41] For further reading see *Mind Games* by Jean Houston and R. E. L. Masters. Wellingborough, Northants: Turnstone Press, 1973, and *Passages: a guide for pilgrims of the mind* by Marianne Andersen and Louis Savary. Wellingborough, Northants: Turnstone Press, 1977.

[42] Charles A. Garfield, 'Conscious alteration and the fear of death' in *Journal of TransPersonal Psychology*, No. 2, 1975.

[43] A. H. Maslow, 'The Plateau Experience' in *Journal of TransPersonal Psychology*, No. 2, 1972.

44 Anthony Bloom, *The School of Prayer*. London: Darton, Longman & Todd, 1970.

45 Lao Tsu, *Tao Te Ching*. Trns. Gia-Fu and Jane English. London: Wildwood House, 1973, verse 15.

46 Al Chung-lian Huang, *Embrace Tiger and Return to Mountain: the essence of T'ai Chi*. Moab, Utah, USA: Real People Press, 1973.

47 'The Katha Upanishad' in *The Upanishads* trns. from the Sanskrit with an Introduction by Juan Mascaro. Penguin Classics, 1965.

48 The account taken from *The Journal and essays of John Woolman* ed. by A. M. Gummere (London: Macmillan, 1922) quoted in *Christian Faith and Practice*, §51.

49 Rainer Maria Rilke, *Duino Elegies* trns. from German by J. B. Leishman and Stephen Spender. London: Hogarth Press, 4th edn., 1963, 'First Elegy'.

50 George MacDonald in *Give us . . . the Quiet Mind*, ed. by Isabel and William Burnett. London: Mitre Press, 1974.

51 John Punshon, *Alternative Christianity* (PHP 245). Wallingford, Pa., USA: Pendle Hill Publications, 1982.

52 Douglas V. Steere, *Mutual Irradiation* (PHP 175). Wallingford, Pa., USA: Pendle Hill Publications, 1971.

53 R. E. L. Masters and Jean Houston, *The Varieties of Psychedelic Experience*. London: Turnstone Press, 2nd edn., 1973, p. 307.

54 Teilhard de Chardin, *Writings in time of war: The Priest*. London: Fontana, 1968, p. 222.

55 Chogyam Trungpa, *Cutting through Spiritual Materialism*. London: Robinson & Watkins, 1973, p. 6.

56 Nicolas Berdyaev, *The Destiny of Man*. London: Geoffrey Bles, 1937, p. 151.

57 Teilhard de Chardin, *Toward the Future*. London: Collins, 1974.

58 Sobhana Dhammasudhi, *Insight Meditation*. Committee for the Advancement of Buddhism, 2nd edn., 1968.

59 Pir Vilayat Inayat Khan, *New Age Meditations*. New York: Winged Heart Press, and *The Message in our Time: the life and teaching of the Sufi master Pir-O-Murshid Inayat Khan*. New York: Harper & Row, 1978.

60 See 'Process Thought and the Philosophy of Whitehead' in *The Darkness of God: theology after Hiroshima* by Jim Garrison. SCM, 1982.

61 John Yungblut, *Speaking as one Friend to Another on the mystical way forward* (PHP 249). Wallingford, Pa., USA: Pendle Hill Publications, 1983.

62 Damaris Parker-Rhodes, *Christianity and the Social Order*. London: Friends Home Service Committee, 1954.

63 Berdyaev, *op. cit.*, p. 281.